BOAT MODELLING

Boat Modelling

Vic Smeed

ARGUS BOOKS

Argus Books Limited
1 Golden Square
London W1R 3AB
England

First published 1956
Sixteenth (completely revised and rewritten) edition 1985
Reprinted 1986

© Argus Books Ltd 1984

ISBN 0 85242 848 0

Phototypesetting by Photocomp Ltd

Printed and bound by A. Wheaton & Co. Ltd, Exeter

Contents

Introduction

When 'Boat Modelling' was first published in 1956 it was little thought that it would appear in other languages and that, with periodic up-datings, it would run to fifteen English impressions and still be in print and in demand twenty-five years or so later. In that time it had introduced many thousands of readers to the pleasures of model boating and quite a number were kind enough to write to tell of successful models, some of which had won competitions, built solely from information gleaned from the book.

However, time moves on and although essential matters had been kept in step with progress, some aspects of the book were becoming sufficiently dated as to lose their value, and when the last impression had sold out it was decided not to go ahead with a further reprint. Demand nevertheless continued to be strong and continual, and it therefore seemed proper to revise and rewrite the material in the light of 1980s practice and to reintroduce the book under the same title and with the same general approach but in a modernised form. Literally a case of 'by popular request'!

Some of the words and many of the line illustrations are as valid now as they were originally, but most sections have been amended, added to or totally rewritten with developments and further experience as a guide, and the opportunity has been taken to introduce useful photographs throughout the pages rather than concentrated on inserted plates as in the original edition. Among valid comments in the original are the introductory words 'I cannot see one subject on which I would not like to have written more', which still applies, but then so does the original aim, which was a compact, practical and useful book providing comprehensive coverage of a very large subject; there are nowadays other books treating individual aspects in greater detail once a reader has determined his area of interest. From the thousands of copies sold, the original book seems to have been found useful and it is hoped that this new edition will prove equally successful in encouraging newcomers in their first steps in this fascinating hobby. Whether it, too, will still be in demand in another 25 years, or what indeed will be being built and sailed in 2010 we have no means of knowing, but as long as it stretches imagination and skills and brings people together in enjoyable pursuits it must be worth doing.

Vic Smeed

Chapter One

A Look at the Subject

The expression 'model boats' covers an astonishingly wide field. On the one hand are the small power craft and yachts seen at almost any time in the hands of youthful owners at the local park pondside, and on the other are the enthusiasts' highly efficient racing machines and the research models which contribute so much to technical advances in the full-size world. Between these extremes lies a fascinating selection of classes — so many that it is perhaps advisable to group them as conveniently as possible at the outset of this book.

Power Craft
There are various forms of power plant in common use, and various types of boats to use them; practically any combination can be used, so let us first examine the available means of power.

(i) *Electric.* More model boats use this form of power than any other, and enormous progress has been made in both motors and power supplies in recent years. Installations can be simple, inexpensive motors running off dry batteries (a diminishing source of power due to cost) through to extremely powerful specialised motors using banks of nickel-cadmium cells, capable of providing speeds equalling all but the very fastest internal-combustion engined boats. Electric power is clean, cool, quiet and reliable and uncomplicated to use in the average model and, unlike i.c. engines, running in reverse is simple. The chief disadvantage can be short running time per charge (10-20 minutes) but cells for rapid recharging from a car battery are easily available.

(ii) *Petrol (spark ignition).* For larger models, since almost all available two-strokes and four-strokes are in the bigger capacities. The weight, complication and cost of the ignition equipment puts them at a disadvantage in smaller sizes, but they are very cheap to operate and speed control is excellent. Not really widely used.

(iii) *Diesels.* More correctly 'compression ignition' engines, these are suited to smaller models, the largest capacity usually being 5cc. Simple to use, with only fuel and a starting cord required, there is a tendency for them to throw out a lot of oily fuel, especially off the flywheel, and steps are needed to prevent fuel soakage into the hull structure. Speed control on smaller motors is only fair, but from 1½cc upward can

A group of scale models including four fire-fighting vessels used by a young German demonstration team for an exciting display.

be very good. Commonly used in Europe and Australasia but rarely elsewhere.

(iv) *Glowplug.* Almost universal for the major speed classes of competition, but also used extensively in all launch-type models. A suitable battery or accumulator is needed for starting, and glowplugs can burn out. Speed control usually good, but protection against fuel seepage and paint attack is needed.

(v) *Steam.* The earliest form of power, steam engines have never disappeared and have seen something of a revival recently, due to cheapness of operation and the nostalgia factor. Most commercial units are small and simple; more powerful plant tends to require fairly high initial investment, though many model engineers make their own. Speed control/reversing is not easy unless the engine includes fairly complex valve gear and, preferably, more than one cylinder. Bulk and weight are significant factors for the amount of power produced, but speeds of over 100 k.p.h. are possible with specialised units.

(vi) *Rubber motors,* once a cheap source of power capable of a 3-4 minute run at moderate speed or a short high-speed dash, are virtually extinct.

(vii) *Clockwork,* though still used for toy boats, is also a thing of the past for 'serious' use. The gramophone motors which used to be converted are now collectors' items in their original form.

(viii) *Jet motors* of the impulse type were tried in the 1950s but nothing significant with either these or turbine types has been achieved. The small solid fuel Jetex motors (effectively a form of rocket motor) have not been produced for many years but in any event give only a few seconds of power per charge.

Types of Boats

It is rather difficult to draw an exact line between some classes of models, but the following list embraces the entire range in general terms.

(i) *Sports models* – usually semi-scale in appearance but simple in construction, may be powered by any of the above forms of propulsion. Size varies from a few inches to five or six feet, but two to three feet overall is most popular.

(ii) *Semi-scale models* – the definition of 'semi-scale' is normally a model which, if scaled up, could conceivably be a seaworthy full-size craft. The expression 'near-scale' is usually applied to a model based on a prototype but usually simplified. Such models constitute the great majority of the small craft afloat today, and can resemble any type of vessel from launches to liners or warships. Most forms of power apply.

(ii) *Scale models* – may be accurate representations of any size of virtually anything afloat. Electric power is most frequently used, except for fast launch types, when an i.c. engine is normal.

(iv) *Straight-running models* – usually long and slim, can be functional, semi-scale or scale. Their aim is to maintain a straight predetermined course, which sounds far easier than it is! Most forms of power are suitable; i.c. engines and steam are much more common in England than in Europe, where electric predominates. Length of such boats is likely to be four to five feet though some scale models are twice this.

(v) *Airscrew hydroplanes* – should only be run with great care since they present a hazard to well-meaning 'helpers' who fail to realise that there is a propeller on top. Can be very simple and no complicated drive is involved. Tethered models can be very fast – over 250 k.p.h.

(vi) *Hydroplanes* – for many years run tethered with spark ignition or glow engines (occasionally flash steam) achieving speeds of up to 200 k.p.h., but a specialised field requiring patience and

Fig. 1 General nomenclature.

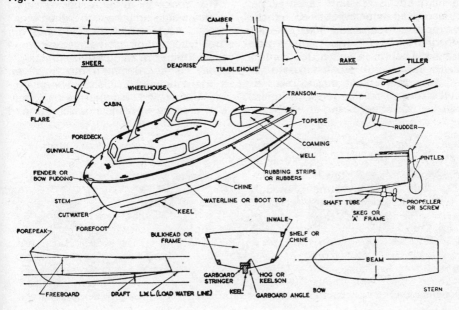

skill. In U.S.A. radio hydroplanes have been operated for many years and there has been some recent interest in other countries. R/C models can reach about 120 k.p.h. on the straight and use glow engines almost exclusively.

(vii) *Special models* – submarines, semi-submersibles, auxiliary sailing vessels and unorthodox models in general are operated for sport and experimentation, appealing to modellers who like to get away from convention.

(viii) *Radio-controlled models* – by far the most numerous, and can be almost any of the foregoing categories. In the 1980s, the most popular choices are electric-powered scale or quite fast i.c. engined launch types 27-40 inches in length.

Sailing Craft

Most sailing models nowadays are Bermuda rig racing yachts, frequently with radio control of sails and rudder, though vane-steered boats are still widely used for racing and there is a growing tendency towards more scale-like appearance. However, the very nature of sailing craft makes accurate scaling down a problem, due to the 'cube law' – one dimension reduces linearly, two by the square, and three by the cube. Thus a ¼ full-size model will be ¼ the length, ¹⁄₁₆ the sail area (¼ long × ¼ high) and ¹⁄₆₄ the displacement (¼ beam × ¼ depth × ¼ length) and its stability will be much reduced as a result. For this reason model yachts are normally designed as stable sailing vessels in their own right where performance is the primary consideration.

Scale models of square-riggers, etc., are built and sailed, but rarely without some form of compromise, usually in the form of a false keel attached for sailing purposes, and even then very little sail can be carried in strong winds. Except for experts the best choice is a large-scale model of a small prototype. Sailing dinghies and other small craft relying on shift of crew weight for stability will almost certainly need a central fin carrying ballast weight, both for stability and to prevent excessive leeway.

The tendency to follow sound model yacht design practice rather than exact scale is explained by the foregoing, but the inclusion of cabins, cockpits and scale fittings on an otherwise functional model is a growing trend. However, model fore and aft sails need booms for efficient setting, a departure from full-size practice in respect of the jib, and

Below, left, a Russian hydroplane capable of about 200 k.p.h. Centre, a British airscrew hydroplane, shown being launched at right. Fastest so far is 161 m.p.h., nearly 260 k.p.h.

Top left, a model of Turbinia *about to score an inner at a M.P.B.A. event, bottom left five multi-racers travelling at 80-90 k.p.h., right a scale ferry docking at the end of its run.*

jibs extending aft of the mast (e.g. a genoa) are not practical when it comes to changing tack.

The recognised classes for model racing yachts, extending from 36in. length to 7-8ft., are detailed in an appendix; 36in. is sometimes considered to be the smallest practical size to sail well, anything much smaller being unable to cope with really strong winds. Sport sailers, able to sail in up to, say, 10 m.p.h. (16 k.p.h.) breezes, can be smaller, and there is one popular kit of only 17½in. length which is used with radio for fun sailing and less serious racing in light winds.

Competitions

The normal competitions for model power boats are also listed in an appendix, but basically they break into three

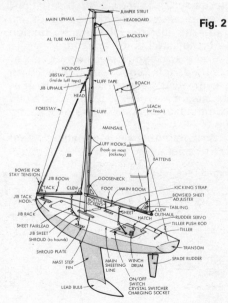

Fig. 2

Ten-rater yachts, vane steered, awaiting the starter's whistle. This is the fastest of all the yacht classes.

categories, each of which is sub-divided into classes. The categories are tethered hydroplanes, straight runners and radio models, for which the international classes are well defined (see Appendix 2). There are often variations used in particular countries, and British clubs may use the following in addition to those listed in the appendix.

Tethered hydroplanes — 30cc, or steam-driven boats (normally flash steam) restricted to 16lbs weight. 15cc or steam to 8lbs. 10cc (hand-built/commercial engines separate) or steam up to 5lbs.

Straight runners — nomination, where the skipper states the time his boat will take to cover a 60-80 yard course, passing through a finishing 'gate', and his score is percentage difference between actual and nominated time. Steering, 3-5 runs using 6 buoys 3½ft apart scoring 1, 3, 5, 3 and 1. Knock-out steering, where top-scoring boats on this course carry on to further rounds until a winner emerges. Such events need a reliable boat capable of running straight, with consistent machinery (different engine

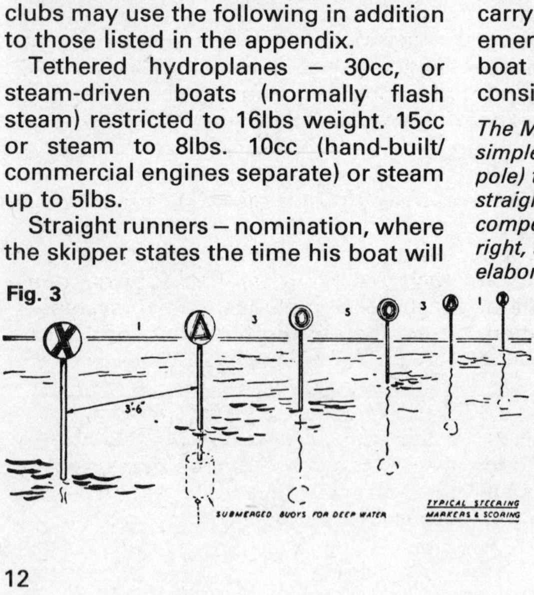

The M.P.B.A. use a simple six-buoy (or pole) target line for straight running competitions. Fig. 4, right, shows the more elaborate Naviga course.

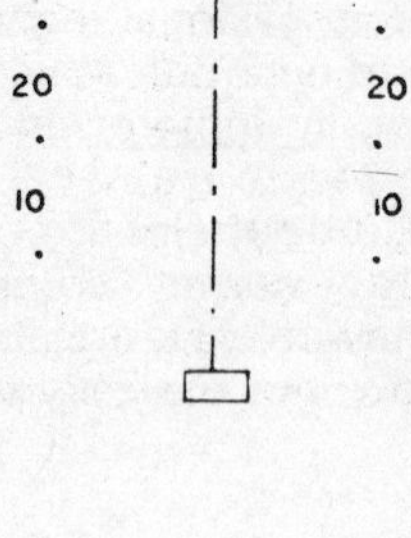

Fig. 3

SUBMERGED BUOYS FOR DEEP WATER

TYPICAL STEERING MARKERS & SCORING

Fig. 4

Six RA class yachts heading for the windward mark in a radio race. These are the biggest yachts raced.

revs. will cause the boat to veer) and an ability to assess wind and current effects

Radio boats – variation of duration of multi-racing events (e.g. 1 hour or 2 hour heats), a class for scale models built from kits, different steering events using non-standard courses, and sometimes calling for scale models to perform scale manoeuvres, offshore racing, where boats are run in the open sea or large lakes with their skippers following in fast ski-boats, record meetings for speed in a straight line (two opposite runs) or round a 440 yard oval, and many other forms of competition.

Sailing Competitions

The only competitions for yachts are races, but for scale-type models there are occasional regattas where less than out and out speed or racing tactics count. Some of these simply judge the impression given by the model afloat as part of a total of points, most of which are awarded for work, etc., but others may involve simple course sailing or a circuit of the lake, passing between the bank and a moored buoy at four or five places.

Yacht racing with vane gear requires each yacht to race every other the length of the lake to windward and return to leeward, 3 points for the windward leg and 2 for the run, i.e. racing is in pairs and a new opponent is met each time. This is the only form of racing models in which spinnakers are regularly carried on the run, the method of racing allowing time for rerigging between each beat and run.

Radio yachts normally sail in heats of 6 to 12 boats, using a count-down to start and racing rules virtually identical to those in full-size use. Points are totted up and a normal race means each yacht having to sail half a dozen times or more. Sometimes a 'fleet' system is used, the bottom two boats of each of three or four fleets moving down to the next fleet and the top two of that fleet moving up at the end of each heat. Match racing, where yachts each meet every other on a one-to-one basis, is not normally encountered but does occasionally occur.

13

Chapter Two

Tools and Materials

The number of tools required to build a model boat will vary considerably with the individual as well as with the type of model under construction. For this reason the following are lists of more or less minimum requirements – some builders will, no doubt, make do without some items, while others will be able to work better with additional tools not mentioned here.

For the average, simple hard chine launch type, the following are suggested. (1) Small tenon saw – there is an excellent 7in. saw with a hand-brush type of handle available cheaply in multiple stores. (2) Junior hacksaw (Eclipse) for both wood and metal cutting. (3) Fret-saw. (4) Small plane. (5) ½in. chisel. (6) Light hammer. (7) One or two screwdrivers. (8) Hand-drill, three or four assorted drills, and a rose countersink. (9) Pliers, preferably taper-nose. (10) One or two small G-cramps. (11) Try-square. (12) Sharp knife or single-edged razor blades.

No more tools than this are required for planked hulls, although a marking gauge is handy if you are used to using one, and one or two files, and even a rasp, may save a lot of glass-papering. Carved hulls get a bit more towards the real carpentry outfit, and besides the above list it is useful to have:

(13) Assorted chisels. (14) Assorted gouges – two or three different sizes are enough. (15) Spoon gouge, about ¾in. (16) Carpenter's brace and assorted bits, especially a 1in. size. (17) Calipers. (18) Spokeshave.

For large models, a bow-saw and a jack-plane are helpful, but most builders will be able to assess their requirements when studying plans for the proposed model. A useful tool is an Abrafile, which will cut in any direction, and is used mounted in a hacksaw frame. Other handy gadgets can be made in the workshop; one example is the simple cramp in Fig. 6. This is made up from two lengths of studding (screwed rod) to which are fitted two strips of wood adjusted up and down by nuts, preferably wing-nuts. Several of these cramps will be needed for a bread-and-butter hull.

Power tools which may be of help are a bandsaw, power fretsaw or jigsaw and possibly a belt sander, used with care. There are jobs where a power plane, a pillar drill and even a lathe may save effort, but none of these is essential. A bench jigsaw or power fretsaw is

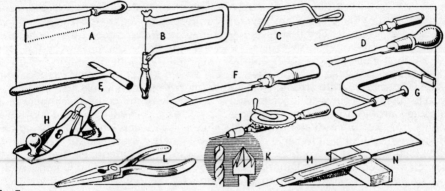

Fig. 5

Tools above are basic, those on right a little more elaborate for carved hulls.

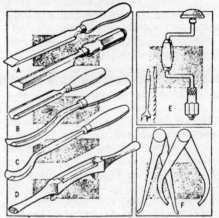

the most useful and the busy builder would save money and time if he then considered a small circular sawbench rather than any of the other power tools listed.

Needless to say, all pins, nails, or screws which will remain part of the structure must be rustless; brass is the normal material for these, though some very fine pins are made only in copper. The most useful type of brass pin is known as a 'gimp' pin, and should be available in sizes from ¼in. up. It has a flat head of nearly ¹⁄₁₆in. diameter, and is thus not so prone to pulling through as brass veneer or panel pins.

Screws used are normally those with countersunk heads, and when a screw is driven in, it pays to follow the correct method by drilling a clearance hole for the shank and a thread hole to provide adequate bite for the thread without the risk of splitting the work.

Really small brass or copper pins are hard to obtain and, with modern adhesives, not really necessary. Steel dressmakers' pins and 1in. veneer pins are a help in holding parts, but are withdrawn

once the glue has set; if a permanent reinforcement is needed trennals can be used. These are made by splitting up a bamboo cane and drawing the strips through successively finer holes in a piece of ⅛in. steel plate to make tiny dowelling. A hole is drilled in the work, the end of a strip dipped in glue, pushed into the hole and snapped off.

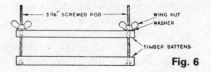

Fig. 6

15

A wide variety of glues now exists, and for boatbuilding there are several specialised products. The first essential is insolubility in water, which rules out such things as Scotch or other animal glues. Some cellulose cements are excellent for work with balsa; harder woods need the slow-drying cements such as Durofix; note that cellulose cements are not totally waterproof. Nor are the 'white' and 'yellow' glues, polyvinyl alcohol (PVA) and aliphatic resin, though they require several hours soaking to soften. If they are thoroughly painted or varnished over and the boat is dried after each outing there is little danger of a catastrophe.

The best results are obtained with urea-formaldehyde resins. Some of these (Aerolite, Beetle, etc), are two-part mixes – the resin is applied to one surface and a hardener to the other. The glue commences to cure when the surfaces are brought together, but a short time is available for positioning the joint accurately. Setting time is affected by temperature, but on average is in the order of 4-6 hours. One resin glue (Cascamite One-Shot) is sold in powder form, ready-mixed and requiring only the addition of water to be ready to use. All these glues are effectively water-and heat-proof when set, and they all have the advantage of being gap-filling. This means that when two slightly irregular surfaces are glued, no air-space will remain, since any discrepancies will be filled by the glue. Although the advantages of this are apparent, and the strength of resin glues is enormous, it should not be made an excuse for sloppy workmanship – a top-line boat calls for complete accuracy from start to finish.

Epoxy resins can provide enormous strength, but building an entire boat with them would be extravagant and unnecessary and their use is better confined to areas where other adhesives will not do – metal to wood is one example. Without exception, all adhesives work best on a fresh sanded surface (wood, metal, plastic, etc.), subsequently untouched by fingers and glued as soon after sanding as possible. Even cyanoacrylate ('instant glue') works better thus, and further requires a close fit for adequate strength; it is not widely used in building model boats.

Only best quality paints and varnishes should be used if a reasonable finish and life expectancy is required. A few coppers saved here can spoil the best model, and this includes brushes too. There are several good paints suitable for the purpose, but if possible marine paints should be used. Cellulose is not really suitable, since it tends to sit on the surface and although hard is prone to abrade, or, if water does find its way behind it, blister off. Ordinary oil colours are better, and modern synthetics better still. Polyurethanes are best of all, especially two-pot ones; cheap polyurethanes contain a very low percentages of the resins which give the finish its toughness. Epoxy paints are tough, but are best sprayed on (on no account inhale spray dust from synthetic/resin paints).

Finally, to the all-important subject of timber. Builders of hard chine or diagonal-planked hulls are fortunate, for the most reliable timber of all is resin--bonded birch ply, and it is readily available in all sizes from $\frac{1}{32}$in. up. Occasionally, this may only be found in metric sizes, but the range of sizes is virtually identical and it is close enough to work on the basis of 3mm=$\frac{1}{8}$in.

Note that 'marine' quality ply is not

essential for model work. Anything under 2mm. is likely to be resin-bonded; thicker ply should be checked that it is at least 'exterior grade', though if adequately painted or varnished most modern plywoods will last for several seasons.

Where timber is required in plank form, the position is by no means so happy. You may be lucky in finding a local yard able to supply suitable wood, but nowadays timber is very frequently kiln-dried, and in nine cases out of ten what may look to be excellent material for the job will eventually let you down. For bread-and-butter hulls the amount of 'movement' (from drying out or from residual stresses produced by kiln-drying) is not likely to be serious, but for a planked hull the results can be disastrous. If you cannot buy guaranteed timber locally, send away to one of the model suppliers who can make a special selection through a timber importer; it may cost you a little more, but is well worth it in the long run.

An alternative and possibly even better scheme is to have a look round salerooms and so on, for an old piece of furniture or a door which you can have cut at a sawyers. Timber obtained from such a source is often ideal for planking and laminated keels (¾in. is the normal maximum width for such items). The timbers best suited to model work are Douglas Fir, Silver Spruce, Yellow Pine, Red Cedar, Lime, Hemlock, African Whitewood, and, of course, Mahogany (preferably American). Of these, cedar, yellow pine and mahogany are outstanding, and these woods can occasionally be found at yards dealing in 'reconditioned' timber. The most easily available 'new' timber, not in the foregoing list, is obeche (sometimes 'obechi'), and if thoroughly dried, etc., this is quite suitable for bread-and-butter hulls. It has the added advantages of being easy to work, and, in normal cases, light in weight, so that a hull need not be carved out quite as thin as is sometimes necessary. Another 'new' wood is jelutong, an excellent wood for carving. For detail work, any of the fruit woods is useful, and for stressed items beech is satisfactory. Small sections are often available in ramin, but this wood is heavy and brittle and should only be used if nothing more suitable is available.

Boat-building sizes differ from normal timber sizes for prepared (planed all round) wood. Customarily 1in.×2in. timber refers to the 'sawn' size, and the dimensions are nominal for planed material, which should be ⅛in. undersize, i.e. ⅞in.×1⅞in. in this example. Sizes given in boat-building are finished sizes, i.e. actual sizes after planing. This is important, particularly when working to a lines drawing for bread-and-butter construction, so if you are having timber sawn and prepared for you, be very specific. Many experts have their planks left ¹⁄₃₂in. oversize and plane down to exact size by hand. To ensure constant thickness over several planks, ask for them to be fed through a thicknesser rather than processed on an overhand planer.

In the foregoing, we have assumed average facilities for intending builders. Obviously, a bench and a carpenter's vice are assets, and some modellers may already have power tools at their disposal. However, there is no need to be discouraged if your equipment is limited − a good many championship models have been built on no more than the humble kitchen table!

Chapter Three

Hard Chine Hulls

A hard chine hull is one in which the sides and bottom join to produce an angle, rather than merging gently from one to the other in a curve. The continuous angle, running from near the bow to the stern, is the chine line, and 'hard' in this sense is an old shipwright's expression which, for definitive purposes, can be taken as 'acute'. Hard chine hulls are also known as 'sharpies' or, simply, 'chine boats'.

The beauty of the hard chine is its extreme simplicity and speed in construction, coupled with smaller outlay in money and skill. Little use of the idea is made in the full-size industry for boats of over 120ft. or so in length (although one enterprising firm is now producing flat-bottomed craft with 'sharp corners') since there are certain disadvantages in stability and strength/weight ratio in really big sizes; however, for modelling the advantages far outweigh any disadvantages.

When a boat is placed in the water, it will displace a volume of water corresponding to its total weight (remember Archimedes?). In actual fact, and as a point of interest, approximately 1·8 cu. in. of water weighs about one ounce, so that for example a 5lb. boat will displace 80×1·8 or 144 cu. in. of water. (It is more accurate to work in lbs/cu. in. – 1lb of fresh water equals 27·7 cu. in., 1lb. of salt water 27·0 cu. in. Thus a 5lb. boat will displace 138·5 cu. in. of fresh or 135 cu. in. of salt water). Now, this water is continually displaced as the boat moves along, even at maximum normal speed. If, however, the boat is overdriven, i.e. more power is applied than is needed to maintain maximum normal speed, the boat, by virtue of its shape (without going into a lot of theory) will tend to rise out of the water

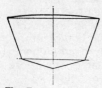

Fig. 7

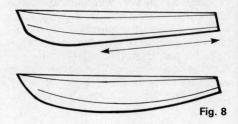

Fig. 8

Fig. 7 (left) is a typical hard chine section, Fig. 8 (right) contrasts a flat run with a rockered keel line. Rocker helps turning ability but is not good for high speed.

Fig. 9

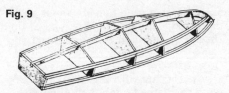

Fig. 10

and begin to 'plane', that is, sit on its stern with its bow out of the water. Part of the boat's weight is supported by lifting forces generated by its movement and the harder the boat is driven the greater is the proportion of weight so supported. The maximum speed of the boat in this condition is considerably higher, of course.

Now, a boat deliberately designed to achieve high speeds above any other considerations must be designed to plane, and a planing boat requires light weight, a flat run (Fig. 8) and a relatively broad transom or stern end, since this is where it will be chiefly supported by the water at speed. The hard chine hull is ideal for these conditions, which is why air/sea rescue launches, motor torpedo boats, and other fast craft employ this system.

A hull designed to make use of such dynamic lift reduces its drag considerably as it rises, allowing greater speed for the same power, or, once planing, the power can be reduced noticeably without loss of speed. The hull shape, however, must be such that it remains stable, and the necessary shape is not altogether 'sea-kindly' when the boat is forced by heavy weather to run at

displacement speed or less.

Lift can be increased by the use of built-in 'spray strips', which are downward-angled, sharp cornered sections built into the chine lines and were first introduced in the author's *Pirana* design in 1960, since when they have become virtually universal for fast models. Another aid to lift is spray rails, parallel sharp-cornered strips arranged in pairs along the hull bottom, or part of it. Initially these were used in full-size simply to stiffen the bottom panels, but their hydrodynamic effect became noticeable as deep vee monohedron (constant deadrise angle) hulls were developed for offshore racing. Such hulls, widely used for multi-racing models (where the water tends to get very choppy) tend to rise and travel on an area of water between a pair of rails, but the rail positions and lengths are fairly critical for performance increase, rather than a drop in speed and turn stability brought about by drag from incorrectly positioned rails. Finding the best positions/lengths for a new design is, like much else in model power boating, a matter of experiment.

The disadvantages of the hard chine are more apparent in sailing craft. Given sufficient wind, yachts will plane on the run, but working across or into the wind (reaching or beating) calls for

Fig. 11

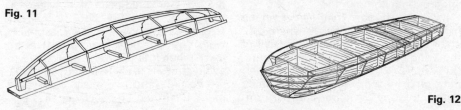

Fig. 12

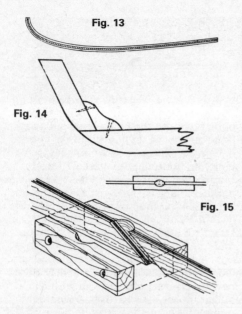

Fig. 13

Fig. 14

Fig. 15

hull characteristics in which the chine hull does not noticeably shine; chief among these is the necessity to sail at a slight heel (the 'sailing angle') and chine boats refer to be sailed upright. Even so, the principal reason for the absence of hard chine hulls in full-size sailing is that the rules frequently preclude them; there are, of course, special classes (e.g. Star' and 'Cadet') which are for chine boats only. On the model side, the windward work of sharpies puts them slightly at a disadvantage, although such boats have finished in the top half-dozen in more than one international competition.

It will thus be seen that the hard chine is excellent for power boats, where constant power is available irrespective of the wind, but may have slight limitations for sailing craft. For a beginner, the simplicity of construction frequently outweighs any limitations in perform-

ance, so that whether power or sail is preferred, a boat with this type of hull should be first choice for a novice.

Construction

The basic hull of a sharpie at its simplest consists of five longitudinal members – a central keel, two chines (sometimes called 'chine stringer' or 'shelf') and two inwales (Fig. 9) to form the remaining two corners of a pentagon – plus a number of lateral members ('frames' or 'bulkheads') and a stem and stern. There are two methods of producing this basic assembly (a) by making the keel member a jig to which the bulkheads are fitted, or (b) by erecting the bulkheads in a separate jig (upside down), and adding the keel, chines, and inwales, removing the jig at a later stage in the building schedule. Which of these two basic methods is adopted depends on whether the bulkheads are to remain a permanent part of the finished hull.

The average power boat is built up as a complete structure, with all the components added during building remaining part of the finished model. Usually this means a fairly generous keel member upon which the bulkheads can be fitted and aligned positively, but occasionally 'egg-box' construction is used (Fig. 12). In this, two longitudinal built-in jigs receive the bulkheads, each item being slotted so that positive alignment is assured. Light inwales, chines, and keel are added before planking or skinning. An advantage of this system is that an accurate hull can be built by anyone able to wield a saw reasonably well. With a single keel care must be taken when fitting inwales and chines to avoid stresses likely to lead to an asymmetric hull, and it is best to fit these members in their respective pairs.

20

Breaking the assembly into detail, let us examine the most popular form of power boat hull. The first item is the keel, and the modern scheme is to cut this from ply. At one time the keel and stem were fashioned in one piece from a grown crook, but with ply this is unnecessary, since the stem can be cut as part of the keel. Occasionally a laminated keel/stem is used, particularly where a gentle curve exists at the bow, and this is made from thin strips glued together under pressure (see Fig. 13). Another method is to cut the stem and keel from timber of ⅜in. thickness or more, making a glued joint reinforced by brass pins or screws and a 'knee' cut from the same timber (Fig. 14).

With the normal single-screw boat, the propeller shaft must pass through the keel. There are two types of shaft, that which is enclosed in a tube for the whole of its length, and that which runs 'in the open' and is provided only with a short 'stuffing box' to provide a bearing and a seal where it enters the hull. The tube type has a bush at each end only, so that the diameter of the tube is rather greater than the shaft diameter; as an example, a ³⁄₁₆in. shaft is normally found in a ⅜in. o.d. tube. Exposed shafts are usually fitted to racing designs or very fast boats where a universal joint is required, but for the average boat the full-length tube is quite satisfactory.

The problem of passing a ⅜in. tube through a keel which may be only ⅛in. thick is overcome by fitting blocks on either side (Fig. 15). A strip is cut out of the keel at exactly the right angle and width for the shaft, and the two parts pinned accurately in place over the plan. One block is now glued in place and left to dry thoroughly, following which the assembly may be lifted and

A monohedron moderate V hull is used on the Lesro Streaker model. Note small spray strips.

the second block glued in place and pinned or screwed through to the other. This is a much more accurate system than endeavouring to drill or burn a hole through after assembly. The tunnel in the blocks may be drilled with the channel in the ply as a guide, but it is better to chisel and file each block before glueing in place. A close fit is not absolutely essential, since any gaps will later be filled with paint-soaked cotton waste rammed in tightly.

When a thick keel is used and it is necessary to drill a shaft tunnel (an operation usually performed at a late stage of assembly) much trouble can be avoided by making a simple jig as in

Fig. 16

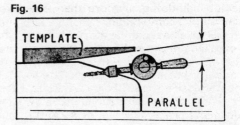

TEMPLATE

PARALLEL

Fig. 17

Fig. 16. The length of hole to be drilled is usually considerably greater than that of a standard drill, and unless a special long-shanked auger bit is purchased or a standard drill silver-soldered to a length of rod it is advisable to burn a pilot hole through with a red-hot wire (about 12 s.w.g. is adequate). This hole can then be followed from both ends and a rat-tail file used to finish the tunnel off.

It is common for the keel assembly to project slightly beneath the completed boat, i.e. the planking or bottom skin butts against the keel side. To assist in making a good joint, some provision is usually made for seating the skin, and although the keel can be rebated for this, it is much simpler to glue and pin a stringer in place on each side of the keel before assembly. These need only be ⅛in. square. On some designs the bottom skin panels 'overlap' the keel, butting against each other to form a smooth V along the whole length; this merely entails chamfering of the actual keel to suit (Fig. 17).

The bulkheads or frames are glued in place on the keel assembly (still considering the average model) and the joints may be halved to ensure correct positioning. Where a bulkhead is simply notched to receive the keel, skewed pins can be driven through to strengthen the joint.

When all bulkheads and transom are in position and dry, the inwales and chines may be positioned. There is frequently a sharp curve towards the bow, particularly with the inwales, and this is sometimes sawn to shape from flat material. Where a single strip is used, it may be necessary to steam or soak the curve in, and in this case it is advisable to pin or strap the strips in place temporarily and allow them to dry before glueing and pinning permanently. Wetting tends to swell the wood and on drying a contraction of ⅛in. is quite to be expected in a 3ft. length; this is enough to pull the structure severely out of shape. The best method is undoubtedly to laminate chines and inwales from two or three more easily bent strips, glueing along the whole length. This also reduces splitting if pins are driven through when attaching the skin. When the glue is dry, plane off the strips to their correct sections. If sufficiently long strips of material are not available, scarf two or more strips

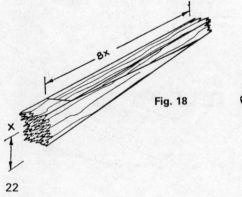

Fig. 18

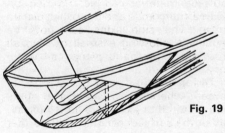

Fig. 19

together, the ideal joint line extending over a distance of eight times the width of the material (Fig. 18). Place such joints at points of little stress, i.e. where the curve is slight. When skinned, no difference in strength will be noticeable.

The entire framework should now be examined carefully for truth. Sight along centre lines for symmetry, above and below, and check that no twist has crept in. Any internal details such as motor mounts, etc., that must be fitted before the hull is planked should be attended to before proceeding further.

It is customary to 'plank', 'skin', or 'cover' the underside of the hull first, and the usual method is to cut thick brown paper or thin card templates to the approximate shape. The inner (garboard) edge is all that need be accurately fitted, and an overlap of about ¼in. is all that need be left on the other edges. After the template is satisfactory, cut the ply and fit the garboard edge accurately by taking a fine shaving or two off with the plane to produce the slight chamfer necessary. Glue all the contacting surfaces, position the ply, and drive in pins, either as permanent fixtures, or to provide temporary pressure while the glue dries. In the latter case, hardened steel dressmakers' pins, pressed in at an angle with pliers, are ideal.

When the glue is thoroughly dry the surplus material can be trimmed off with a sharp knife and the edges planed flush. The side skins can now be attached, allowing a small overlap all round, trimmed and planed off when dry.

Fitting the ply skins is not difficult except where sharp changes of angle are required or excessive flare (concavity of the surface) occurs. In the former case the only really sharp change is at

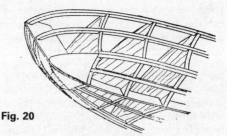

Fig. 20

the boat's forefoot, and it is customary to fit solid blocks at this point (Fig. 19) or to plank the extreme bow with narrow vertical strips. Flare can usually be induced into ply by steaming or slight damping, or even leaving the cut sheet in a tray of wet sawdust for a few hours. In extreme cases narrow vertical strips can be used, and a sheer stringer let into the bulkheads mid-way between inwale and chine facilitates this (Fig. 20). Sometimes the extreme bow is built up from vertical strips of timber around ¼in. thick, the flare being carved in when the glue is dry.

With a fine bow, the angle between side and bottom skins can flatten out over a distance, and when it gets to

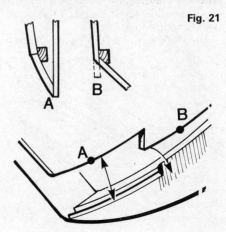

Fig. 21

about 160° the amount to be chamfered off the bottom skin to seat the side becomes excessive. At a convenient point, therefore, the overlap can be stopped abruptly and the joint between the skins forward of this point made a plain butt joint along the centre of the chine stringer (Fig. 21). This requires a little more care in fitting both skins but provides a much neater finish. Usually the bottom skin can be glued on and the joint line carefully pared down with the help of a flexible steel rule and a sharp

Fig. 22
Diagonal planking

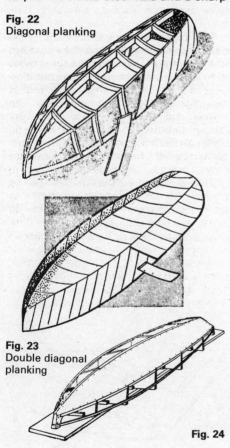

Fig. 23
Double diagonal planking

Fig. 24

knife, but the side skin must be fitted accurately on this joint before glueing. The fact that overlap can be allowed along deck, chine and transom makes this less critical.

Some scale models may have flare running along the entire hull, sides and bottom. In such a case diagonal planking is frequently employed; this is a simple method and, if double diagonal planking is used, results in a remarkably strong hull. For most models the ply or timber can be cut into long strips 1in. wide; the end of the strip is laid in place somewhere amidships, at an angle of 45° to the fore-and-aft line, marked off, and cut to length. A small overlap can remain if required. This strip is now glued and pinned in place (a sheer stringer running the length of the boat is desirable) and another strip laid up to it, cut, fitted, and so on, until the entire surface is planked. Double planking means laying on the second set of planks at right angles to the first. This system, using ⅟₃₂in. (·8mm) ply for each 'layer', is excellent for strong, light hulls up to 48in. in length.

Before decking, the interior of the hull requires painting (see Chapter Nine). After painting and completion of internal detail, the deck, suitably cut for hatches, etc., can be glued and pinned in place, completing the basic hull.

A hard chine hull can, of course, be built without permanent bulkheads, and yachts with such hulls are usually built in this fashion. The 'shadows' employed are more or less bulkheads which are later removed, and the essential difference in that the hull is built upside down on a jig in much the same manner as a planked hull. Reference to the next chapter will fill in the details of the following outline procedure.

Shadows in an edge-on jig with a pair of dowels to check truth at all stages. Clips, pegs and clamps hold one bottom skin in place while the glue dries.

The shadows are cut with sufficient material left above the inwale line to bring their top edges to a straight line. All required notches are cut for keel, chines, and inwales, and the shadows, stem, and transom are then erected on a jig board at their correct stations. The fore and aft members are added and lightly pinned in place (they can, of course, be glued to stem and transom) and the resulting frame skinned as previously detailed. Care must be taken to glue the skin only to the permanent structure. When dry, a rigid assembly remains, which can be cleaned up externally with complete safety. The assembly is then removed from the jig and the shadows twisted out. Deck beams, etc., can be added as each shadow is removed to reduce any chance of the hull springing out of shape.

The big advantages of hard chine hulls are that they are simple and quick to build, light in weight, and, of course, they offer little difficulty in timber supplies. Ply is the main material, and is reasonably easy to buy anywhere. The chines, etc., can be made from any long-grained wood, and spruce should be available in any respectable model or handicraft shop. Several of the author's models have been built using planed pine laths sawn in half (giving about $\frac{3}{16} \times \frac{3}{8}$in., 6-7ft long) or $\frac{1}{2} \times 1\frac{1}{2}$in. doorstop (actually $\frac{3}{8}$in. thick) sawn into three or four strips. Failing this, obeche can be used if no better choice lies to hand; some of the exotic timbers imported – sanga, meranti, quaraba, etc., are perfectly suitable for such purposes if thoroughly dry and free from twist or other defects.

Chapter Four

Round Bilge Hulls

Most full-size craft have 'round bilge' hulls, the 'bilge' being the part of the hull between the 'floor' and the 'side'. When the floor curves gently into the side the hull is of the round bilge type; softening the turn of the bilge means making the curve flatter, and hardening the turn is the reverse, terminating, of course, in the 'hard chine' when a definite chine or corner exists.

A very high proportion of model boats do, of course, follow full-size prototypes to a greater or lesser extent, which means that the round-bilge hull

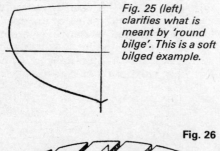

Fig. 25 (left) clarifies what is meant by 'round bilge'. This is a soft bilged example.

Fig. 26

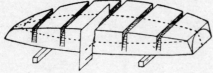

is common in the model world. Most model yachts employ a rounded hull, too, since there are hydrodynamic advantages in this shape. At one time if was normal to carve such a hull out of one solid lump of timber, and for small hulls this may still be done (Fig. 26 gives the easiest system). However, the two main systems used nowadays are much easier and more economical; these are the bread-and-butter and rib-and-plank methods.

Bread and Butter

In this system the bread is the timber and the butter the glue used to bond the planks together. There are two separate methods, bread and buttering on the waterlines, and bread and buttering on the buttocks. To explain these we must look at a typical lines drawing of a hull as prepared by a naval architect; a small scale reproduction is shown in Fig. 27. Looking at the profile of the hull, it will be seen that the shape is divided into equal 'slices' by horizontal lines. These are the waterlines, and they are shown in full on the plan view of the hull just below. If timber of the same thickness as the 'slices' is cut into a number of planks, each shaped to one

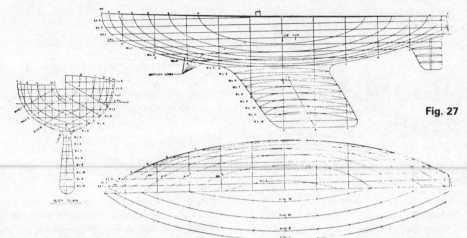

Fig. 27

of the waterlines, an embryo hull is immediately achieved. It will be apparent that all but the bottom plank can have much of the centre removed before assembly; an accurate assessment of the required inner line can be made by sketching the structure and wall thickness over the body plan (the third part of the drawing) as in Fig. 29. If this is done on each section shown on the body plan, a series of points can be marked on the planks which when connected will give an inner line to saw to. Lower planks can frequently be cut from the inner parts of the upper planks to economise on materials.

The second method also uses the lines given on the drawing, in this case the parallel fore-and-aft lines dividing

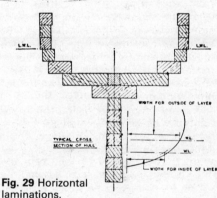

Fig. 29 Horizontal laminations.

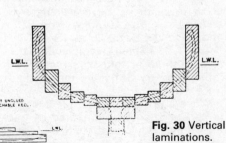

Fig. 30 Vertical laminations.

Fig. 28 B & B on the waterlines.

Fig. 31 Use of templates.

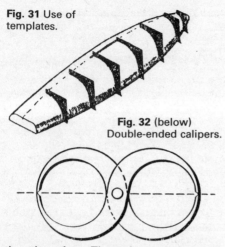

Fig. 32 (below) Double-ended calipers.

Fig. Holding a hull for outside carving.

Fig. 34 Holding a hull for inside carving.

the plan view. These buttock lines are shown in full as the curved lines on the profile, and the planks will, of course, be vertical and in pairs. The same system of determining how much may be safely cut out can be followed. This method has the advantage that it is easy to check that both sides are absolutely identical, since the joint lines can be used to ensure symmetry; this is of paramount importance.

Whichever method is followed, the procedure is identical. After sawing the planks to shape, they must be thoroughly glued together under pressure. A high-quality glue is essential, as is accuracy in line-up. Several cramps will be needed to provide an even pressure, and these can be made very simply, as detailed in Chapter Two. It is often best to glue three or four planks at a time rather than try to handle the whole at once.

While the glue is drying, a set of templates should be prepared by tracing off the body plan on to thin ply, stiff card, or even thin metal. The outside of the hull is then carved to approximate

shape, using chisel, plane, spokeshave, rasp, etc., and making rough checks with the templates. When the final shape is emerging, accurate pencil lines should be drawn at the template stations to assist the work. Always use the cutting tools 'downhill' on the grain, and never take off huge cuts. Finish this stage with coarse glass-paper, since small scars are likely to be sustained during hollowing the interior and these will be removed in the final glass-papering.

The interior is hollowed by using a brace and bit to drill closely-spaced holes where much material has to be removed. An odd length of tube slipped over the bit shank and taped to the chuck can be used as a depth gauge. The remaining material is pared away with a gouge, again taking light cuts down the grain. It is well worth making a pair of double-ended calipers (Fig. 32) for checking wall thickness as work pro-

Fig. 35 Typical deck beams A, B, D, E, F. C is mast slide support, G for rudder tube.

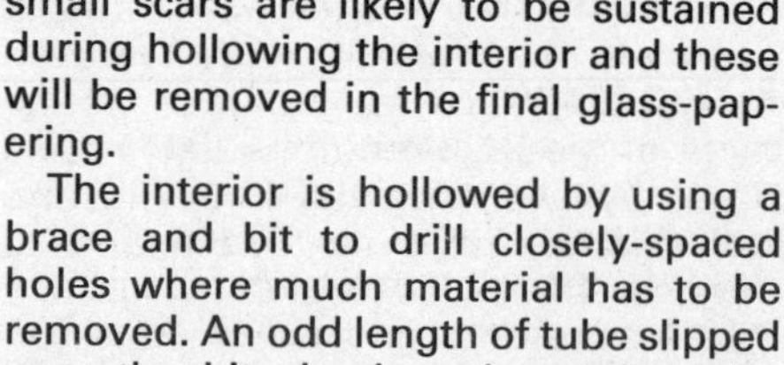

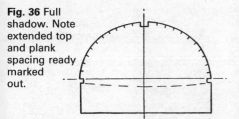
Fig. 36 Full shadow. Note extended top and plank spacing ready marked out.

ceeds. The interior should be finished smooth with successive grades of glasspaper when the designer's specified hull weight is within reach. An electric light bulb inside the hull will often show up areas not yet carved as thin as needed.

Deck-beams and other internal reinforcements should be added (Fig. 35) and the exterior polished up with fine glasspaper before proceeding with the initial painting stages.

Rib and Plank

This system offers a rather lighter hull and is thus possibly more frequently found among model yachts than power boats. Material requirements are a little more stringent, since a finished hull can more easily twist or 'starve' out of shape, but less heavy work is required to build a hull by this method. The following description applies to a yacht hull, but may equally be applied to other craft.

The first requirement is a jig, which may be a flat plank of 1in.×4in. or so, slightly longer than the hull to be built. Occasionally a second piece of timber is screwed beneath the first to form a 'T',

which ensures that the first board cannot assume a curve during building. A straight and accurate centre line must be drawn along the jig.

Shadows, usually of ¼in. ply, are now cut and fitted to the jig. Each shadow is traced off a body section on the body plan, but since these sections show the outside line of the finished hull, allowance must be made for the thickness of the planking and the ribs. Where the shadows will remain as bulkheads in the finished hull, only the planking thickness is allowed for, of course. The shadows are extended at the top so that the extended tops all fall on a straight line (Fig. 36), and they are secured upside down on the jig either by cutting notches in the jig and pinning them in, or by screwing a ½in. square fillet to the top of each and screwing into each fillet from the underside of the jig (Fig. 37). Notches for keel and inwales must be provided in the shadows, and they must be very accurately positioned on the jig.

The keel, stem, and sternpost assembly (the backbone) is next assembled directly over the plan; in the case of a yacht this is normally one smooth sweep of timber, and is best laminated from several strips of ⅛in. material (Fig. 38), the width corresponding to the plank width at the midsection, i.e. ¾in. for A hulls, ⅝in. for 10 Raters and Marbleheads, and ½in. for 36R models, etc. When thoroughly dry, the backbone is dropped in place in the shadows, and the inwales similarly positioned and

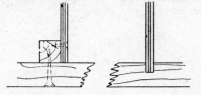

Fig. 38 Backbones may be laminated in jigs made up of small wood blocks, or sawn from the solid.

The first two planks each side are in place on this 36R hull. Ribs are easily visible; note also centre deck stringer and ply fin already positioned.

glued to the stem and transom, either direct, or by means of the breasthook, etc. Blocks, suitably rebated, are usually employed at the extreme bow and stern (Fig. 39).

Usually ¹⁄₁₆in. ply is used for the ribs and this is cut into ¼in. strips fitting round each shadow from the keel to the inwale. A little additional strength may be gained by jointing the ribs into the backbone and inwales, but the most important thing is to see that the ribs are flush with the other members. Temporary pins can be tapped in to hold them to the curve of the shadows. Check alignment by laying a strip of planking in place.

The planks are normally cut from ⅛in. material – slightly thicker for the bigger classes. The planking must be set out on the body plan by stepping off the largest section to the required plank width (see above) and diagonalising as in Fig. 41. Note that most of the planks terminate on the backbone and do not run from end to end. The approximate plank width at each section can be taken off this 'planking plan'.

Mark out two sheer planks (one left and one right if your material is planed on one face only) leaving the top edge straight; make sure that the marks made for the widths at the section stations join in a smooth curve. Cut and plane the curved edge, square to the face, and glue in place (planed face in if not planed both sides). Normally the deck will be screwed on top of the planking, but if you wish to let it in allowance must be made for this. The planks may be pinned in place (some experts use boot-maker's tingles for this), the pins being withdrawn when the glue is dry.

The second pair of planks is now prepared in exactly the same way, except that the top (straight) edges will require the faintest of bevels to fit snug-

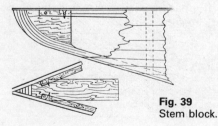

Fig. 39
Stem block.

Fig. 40
Fitting a rib

Fig. 41

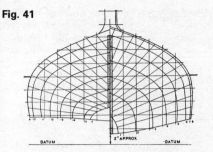

DATUM   2" APPROX   DATUM

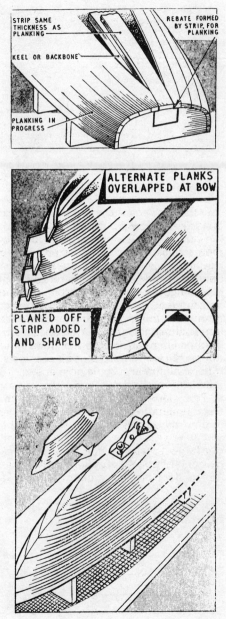

STRIP SAME THICKNESS AS PLANKING

KEEL OR BACKBONE

PLANKING IN PROGRESS

REBATE FORMED BY STRIP, FOR PLANKING

ALTERNATE PLANKS OVERLAPPED AT BOW

PLANED OFF, STRIP ADDED AND SHAPED

ly. Continue in this way. When the after ends of the planks approach the backbone, glue and pin a strip of planking over the backbone, about ¼in. narrower, from the transom to the after end of the deadwood, to form a rebate to receive the plank ends. The forward plank ends are alternately overlapped (Fig. 44) over the backbone, and when all the planking is completed, the 'point' thus formed is planed off to ¼-⅜in. flat and a strip of wood fastened round and planed to correct section. This 'locks' the planks and moreover prevents them splitting if the boat has the misfortune to ride over a hard obstacle.

Most yachts nowadays carry a 'plate' fin shaped from ply or Tufnol, extending through the planking and backbone and carried up to deck level for maximum strength, as in the photograph opposite. The backbone may well require doublers each side to reinforce the slotted length. Yachts with thick fins, however, carry a garboard piece to which the fin butts, with metal rods or keel bolts passing through for internal

Fig. 42
Inset or overlapping deck.

Right, top to bottom, **Figs. 43, 44** and **45.**

31

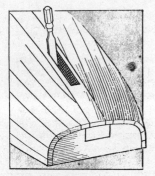

Fig. 46 Chiselling the skeg slot.

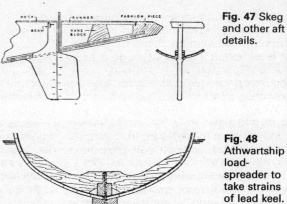

Fig. 47 Skeg and other aft details.

Fig. 48 Athwartship load-spreader to take strains of lead keel.

fastening. When planking is completed the hull must be planed off to receive the garboard piece (Fig. 45) and great care must be exercised to ensure a perfectly true surface. The garboard piece is cut from a single block, and is best fitted by drilling the keel bolt holes through it and the backbone, and bolting together while the glue dries. The piece is then faired into the body and the planking can be cleaned up.

Scrape off any surplus glue and withdraw all pins. Run a plane lightly across the 'corners', and glasspaper with a coarse paper in all directions but more 'round' the hull than along it. Proceed with progressively finer grades of paper, lightly damping the hull to raise softer fibres, until a reasonable surface exists.

Before moving the hull mark out the slot for the skeg, if fitted, and drill and chisel right through the backbone. The skeg itself is cut and fitted in the slot; for additional strength it may run right through to deck level (Fig. 47). Check that the alignment is perfect before glueing permanently in place.

Now remove the building jig, leaving the shadows in place, and bolt the hull to the bench or to a strip of timber held in a vice. Knock or twist out the sha-

The hull in the preceding photo planked, removed from jig and shadows knocked out. Scrap spacers make sure that hull beam remains as designed till deck beams are fitted.

dows, working from ends to middle, and clean up the inside of the hull shell. Any further internal reinforcement must now be added; this is usually limited to load-spreading members designed to distribute the stresses of the heavy lead keel (Fig. 48). A handle is often incorporated for carrying the hull (Fig. 49). At this stage too, the first coat or two of the interior varnish may be brushed on (see Chapter Nine).

The next job is to fit the deck beams. These are cut to length and planed to correct camber (if a cambered deck is employed) from similar material to that used for the inwales. The beams are then halved into the inwales and fitted flush (Fig. 50). These beams are positioned to stiffen the deck and also to provide anchorages for various deck fittings. Fig. 35 shows a typical lay-out.

Ply is normally employed for the deck, and this is cut to shape and cleaned up, but not fitted until the interior is fully varnished, etc. The hatch, however, may be cut and the cover fitted; this is located over the keel fixing bolts and the aperture should be large enough to admit a hand. The hatch cover is normally a rectangle of mahogany, etc., about ¼in. larger all round than the hatch, to which is cemented a plug tightly fitting the hole; this may also be of timber but a better job can be made by using sheet cork.

The remaining job is the fin keel, which if of the ply plate type is best shaped and fitted into the hull before decking (or even before planking), taking great care to ensure that it is vertical and aligned accurately fore and aft. Such a fin will normally carry a lead

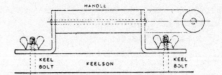

Fig. 49 Internal carrying handle.

Fig. 50 Deck beam/inwale jointing.

bulb, which can be attached as virtually the last step before painting. In the case of scale models or thick-finned racing yachts (still sometimes found in the A, 6m and 36R classes) the fin is a carving exercise, usually from one block of wood but occasionally built up from horizontal laminations.

The entire fin is shaped and later cut to provide the pattern for the lead, which, when cast and cleaned up, is bolted through the remaining portion of the fin (the deadwood) in the manner described in Chapter Eight.

Many types of hull can be built on the rib and plank system, following the general principles outlined above. Most will be simpler; for example, a small trawler hull would use a block stem and counter with planking between, and would require no garboard piece or skeg, etc. Where sharp changes of curvature occur, planking can be difficult, so that the drawings for a proposed model should be carefully considered before deciding on rib and plank construction.

Chapter Five

Other Types of Construction

There are several other systems for building which apply to specific types of hull or to the working facilities available. Many of them are variants or combinations of methods already described, but one or two are completely different.

'Two-shelf' Chine Hulls

It will be obvious that a hard-chine hull is five-sided, the widest 'side' being the deck. If we make the deck a primary structural member in the form of a complete shelf sawn to planshape, and make the chines in the same way, we have only to add a keelson or keel assembly to provide the 'fifth corner' (Fig. 51). Advantages are the ease with which a symmetrical hull is produced,

Fig. 51

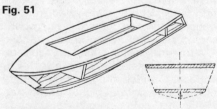

Fig. 52 'Two-shelf' hull

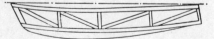

the positive fixing for the ply skins, and the small amount of internal structure necessary. Camber may be planed into the deck, and if pliant timber is used, deck sheer and chine curve can be incorporated by judiciously placed bulkheads and diagonal bracing (Fig. 52). Naturally, the system is not quite scale boat-building, and has its limitations, but for ease of building and overall strength it has much to commend it.

Composite Hulls

Quite a number of full-size ship types lend themselves to the simplified construction shown in Fig. 53, common examples being destroyers and oil tankers. The bow and the stern are the only parts deviating from a squarish cross-section, so these are built up on the bread and butter principle, with the midships portion employing only three planks for the bottom and sides. The thickness of these planks allows for the hull section to be carved in, but when thin planks are used a fillet can be fitted into the corner to preserve strength (Fig. 54).

Thick-bottomed Hulls

In some cases of boats similar to the foregoing, it is possible to use one

Fig. 53

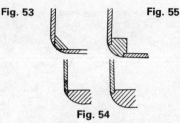

Fig. 55

Fig. 54

Top, fillets, and, above, thick bottom planks.

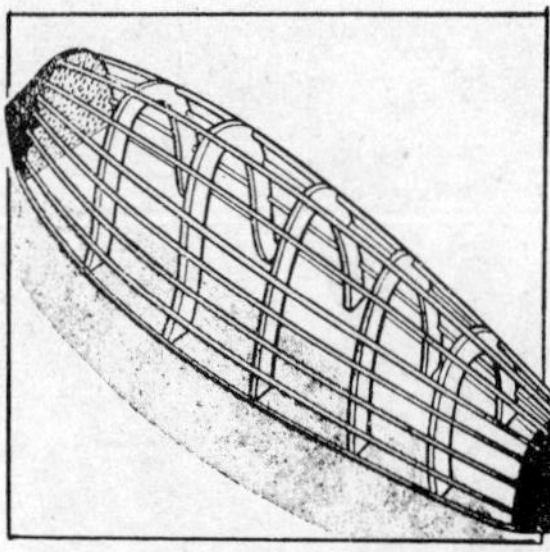

thick plank for the hull bottom and erect ply sides for most of the rest of the hull. The sides normally need to terminate on a bulkhead towards the stern, and the stern itself is then planked on a light frame or even bread-and-buttered. The round of the bilge will determine the thickness of the bottom plank (Fig. 54).

Diagonalled Bilge Hulls

The double diagonal-planking system described in Chapter Two is excellent for round bilge hulls, with or without permanent bulkheads. The one difference in setting up for planking is that stringers are necessary in addition to ribs. These must be flush with the ribs and spaced about 2in. apart, running from the extreme bow to the stern. The planks are laid on in exactly the same manner as for a chine hull, and joined to the backbone in the same way as normal planks. The second layer can be laid on fore and aft instead of diagonally, if preferred, with no measurable effect on the ultimate strength. When applying diagonals, the width is governed by the amount of curvature, i.e. the planks will be narrower at the ends than the centre with an average hull. A trial strip will quickly determine whether the width is too great.

Gum-Strip Hulls

The enormous strength of laminated gum-strip paper is not generally realised. If you require to be convinced, soak a length of good quality gummed brown paper strip and wind it carefully round a broom-handle (over an ordinary sheet of paper so that it will slide off) until it approaches 1/16in. thick. Allow to dry thoroughly or bake the tube in a cool oven for an hour, and then try to collapse it. It can be done, of course, but the force required is quite astonishing.

Hulls can be built of this material quite easily and with very satisfactory results. A very light armature is necessary, and the best way to is to cut ply bulkheads, notch them to receive 1/16in. sq. stringers, and set them up in a jig. The stringers need only be 1/16in. balsa, but they must be spaced no more than 1/2in. apart on sharp curves. A heavier inwale is desirable, since a ply deck will be screwed to this. Thoroughly soak the strip and lay it on round the hull first, then diagonally each way, then fore and aft. Repeat until a good thickness is built up – 1/16in. is adequate for most purposes. Only short lengths need be used, and care should be taken to avoid too many air bubbles. When completely dry, rub the outside down and apply one or two coats of shellac. Rub down again, and shellac five or six times more, rubbing down between each coat. The inside also requires several

35

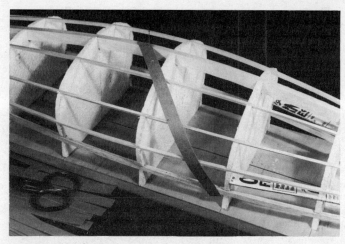

Beginning the first layer of planking (with strips of cereal carton) to make an inexpensive but very successful hull. This 36R yacht proved competitive in national races.

coats of shellac. Varnishing or painting thus has a hard base and is carried out normally. A hull built in this way is a fraction heavier than a wood-planked hull, but a first-class job in every respect.

Papier Mache Hulls

This method is rather a misnomer, since the paper used is not pulped completely. Frankly, it is an evil-smelling process offering little advantage over the previous system except that it is very cheap. Tear a large quantity of old newspapers into squares of 3in. or 4in., and drop them in a bucket of water into which has been dissolved a packet of glue size. They should soak for a day or

so before being used. An armature similar to that described above is needed. Lay the squares of paper in place on the frame until three or four layers have been built up, then allow to dry off slightly. Brush thin glue over ('toffee' glue will do) and add a couple of layers, brush on more glue, add layers, etc., until a thickness of 1/16in. or so has been reached. Finish exactly as above.

Strawboard Hulls

Strawboard is a low-grade type of card, usually grey or fawn in colour, used for packing, etc. Hulls can be built from this material, using it in exactly the same way as timber, and finishing with the shellac process described for the two previous methods. It is particularly suited to diagonal planking and offers the advantages of exceptionally low cost and easy availability of the material. Hulls built of strawboard demand patient workmanship to achieve first-class results, but are extremely strong and seaworthy when finished. Working is simplified by the flexibility of the

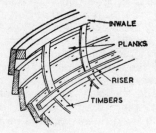

INWALE

PLANKS

RISER

TIMBERS

material when damped.

A similar process can be carried out with card salvaged from cereal cartons.

Clincher Built Hulls

Clincher, or clinker, building, is a system of producing a hull with no internal framework, and incorporates overlapping planks (Fig. 56). Most ordinary wooden rowing boats, dinghies, lifeboats, etc., are built in this way. Procedure is much the same as for normal planked hulls, except that sufficient width must be allowed in each plank for the overlap, and planking must start at the garboard, i.e. next to the keel. In full-size practice the planks are often merely pinned together, but in models it is usual to glue the overlap as well as pinning it. Ply is usually used for planks, since the pins are close to the edge and splitting is frequent with plain timber.

At the bow and stern, the top of each plank is chiselled off to a feather-edge for an inch or two; this allows the next plank to seat down to a nice smooth finish. The pins, projecting inside, are snipped off after completing the planking, and clinched over inside. Timbers are now added (Fig. 56) by pinning through from outside and clinching over. Longitudinal stringers (risers) are added to support thwarts, etc.

Few boats greater than 30ft. or so are built on this system, except for large ships' life-boats and whalers, which may be as much as 70ft. in length.

Fabric Hulls

Occasionally a very lightweight hull may be required, for example for rubber powered speed models. This type of hull can be made by building a hard chine frame of as light construction as will do the job, and covering it with silk or nylon. The material should be applied by soaking in water, blotting lightly in an old towel, and stretching on the frame using pins and a cellulose cement or thick clear dope. The adhesive will 'blush' on contact with the wet fabric, but this will disappear when the material is treated with two or three coats of clear dope and a coat or two of banana oil. Alternatively, two or three coats of varnish may be applied.

Metal Hulls

The production of a metal hull is not difficult provided that the design takes into account the limitations of the material. To arrive at a design and to produce a set of templates, a hull should first be mocked-up in stiff card. Anyone capable of assembling a multi-piece metal hull will be experienced enough to know the limitations of his medium (Fig. 57 shows a typical boat for this type of construction). The beginner is advised to try the two-piece type of hull laid out in Fig. 58. The main section forms the hull itself, and is cut from zinc or lead-coated steel of appropriate

1   HAND RAIL.
2   SLIDING ROOF.
3   CABIN FRONT.
4   MAIN DECK.
5   PORT & STAR'BD SIDE PLATES (CABIN).
6   FOR'ARD BULK'HD.
7   AFT BULK'HD.
8   BOTTOM PLATE.
9   PORT SIDE PLATE (HULL.)
10 STAR'BD   —— ——
11 TRANSOM   PLATE
12 TRANSOM   PLATE (CABIN)

Fig. 57
An 'exploded' sketch of a simple all-metal model.

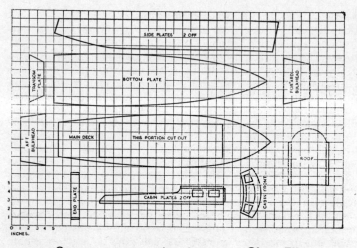

Fig. 57a The simple metal boat above laid out for scaling up. Structure is also suitable for an all-ply model if preferred.

gauge. One or two wooden formers help to achieve the desired 'rolled' shape and these may be permanently installed with screws or later replaced with metal frames. The second piece is the transom, and the assembly is tacked together with solder and cramps and trued up before the final joints are made. These are soldered with the aid of a blowlamp, soft iron wire ($\frac{3}{32}$in. or 12 s.w.g.) being laid inside the corners to help form a fillet. Keel, etc., may be soldered in place, but the deck, motor mounting, etc., are best fitted by means of wood blocks secured to the hull by bolts or screws.

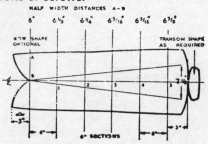

Fig. 58 A 36in round bilge all-metal hull.

Glass Fibre Hulls

Many hulls, particularly for competition and scale models, are nowadays moulded in g.r.p. (glass reinforced plastic, commonly called glass fibre or fibreglass) and quite a large selection can be bought ready-moulded. Advantages (apart from time saved) are strength, interior space, long life without change of weight or shape from water absorption, imperviousness to fuels, etc. and the acquisition of an accurate hull for little more than it would cost to make it in wood. Strangely, the lighter a commercial hull the more expensive it may be, because much more time and care is required to produce it.

Making a pattern, then a mould and then a moulding for a single boat offers no saving in time or cost, but the other advantages are retained and quite a lot of builders think it worthwhile. There is a compromise, and that is to apply a layer of glass and resin to the exterior or interior of a light wood hull; this is known as glass armouring or glass sheathing.

Glass fibres are made up into various

fabrics of varying weight, those of most interest to modellers being woven glass cloth, glass mat (a random agglomeration of strands chopped to about 2in. length) and, occasionally, glass tape, rovings (rather like loosely wound string), and possibly surfacing tissue. Mat is commonest, of 1-2oz. weight. Resins are available in bewildering variety, but only two need concern models, gel coat and laminating resin. The resins bought are supplied with a separate catalyst, mixed in immediately before use, following the instructions on proportions as accurately as possible. Also required is parting agent, usually a watery fluid which can be brushed or sprayed and dries to a very thin film.

For glass sheathing a light hull can be built and may be planked with balsa or other easily-worked wood. The planking, for external sheathing, does not need to be perfect in that small gaps will be bridged. Normally only the exposed coat of resin (the gel coat) is coloured but for external sheathing colour can be added to the whole of the resin (using special pigments from the resin supplier or litho inks) or the resin can be used uncoloured and the hull finished by painting. Care is needed in applying the resin smoothly and rolling it out well in order, firstly, to drive out air bubbles and thoroughly wet the cloth or mat and, secondly, to reduce the amount of rubbing down which will be necessary when the resin has cured.

For sheathing a model, laminating resin is all that is needed. Gel coat resin sets when air is excluded and surfacing resins are available which set only when exposed to air; either may cause problems if not used to specification. Laminating resins will set under most normal circumstances (sometimes slower than the ideal) and will usually remain slightly tacky on the surface. This tackiness disappears with handling, or sanding, or with a quick swab over with cellulose thinners. It sets to a 'green' condition in, usually, 1½-2 hours, when it is tacky, relatively soft, and in the case of a moulding, capable of sagging out of shape. After perhaps 2-3 days it is fully cured, though may still seem tacky. In the green state it is easier to saw to trimmed shape, easier, too, to separate from the mould, but it should be replaced in the mould to cure to avoid risk of permanent distortion. Green resin will rapidly clog abrasive papers.

In all cases, always cut cloth or mat to shape ready for use before handling resin, since it is impossible to avoid considerable stickiness and stopping to clean the hands with thinners or strong detergent every minute or two is not a good idea. Cut and check the glass, then mix the resin and paint on the hull. Lay the glass in place and stipple it down, using the brush with a stencil-type stabbing action. Trying to draw the brush sideways will only ruck up the glass. When the whiteness of the glass turns to semi-transparency it is adequately wetted out. The less resin used relative to the glass content the lighter and stronger should be the result. A coat of fresh resin, perhaps including a filler powder, can be brushed on when the hull is partially set but still tacky. This will make rubbing down easier, once cured.

Internal sheathing is often used to allow a natural wood exterior finish, reinforced and leak-proofed by mat and resin applied to the inside surfaces. It is also used inside old hulls, but this is not as simple as it sounds, since for good results all old paint or varnish must be

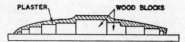

Fig. 59 Making a plaster (or clay) plug.

removed from the interior. No such problem arises with a new hull, and internal fittings may be attached in much the same way as in a shell moulding.

Most g.r.p. hulls are, in fact, shell mouldings formed inside a mould. Since the finished hull surface will reflect the interior shape and finish of the mould and making a female mould from scratch is difficult, the customary process is to make a well-finished pattern or plug and to use this to form a glass-fibre mould in which the final hull will be made. The plug is most often carved from wood, like a bread-and-butter hull, using perhaps old, clean floor boards to laminate the block which, of course, does not need to be hollowed.

Other forms of plug can be made from clay or plaster, by cutting out ply or hardboard sections and mounting them like shadows on a baseboard. Some blocks of wood etc can be fitted in to reduce the amount of clay or plaster required and the latter then trowelled in and roughly smoothed to stand just fractionally proud of the sections. It can then be scraped down to a near-finish (before clay is dry, or when plaster is set but still green), allowed to dry out and then sanded to finish.

With any plug a smooth, glossy and impervious surface is needed and this can be achieved with paint (use emulsion as a primer coat on clay or plaster) or shellac. Remember that the finish achieved will be transferred to the mould and thence to the moulding. Although it is perhaps not essential, a

good hard wax (not silicone) and burnish is often applied as a final step.

The plug should extend ½-1in. or so above the eventual edge line to ensure that a good solid edge can be cut on the finished hull, without risk of airspaces or delamination along the edge. The extension needs to be finished smoothly and treated as the rest of the plug to ensure easy removal of the mould. A line scribed round at the deck-line will leave a visible guide on the mould and hull for sawing off the surplus at the green stage.

Brush-paint or preferably spray parting agent over the whole of the plug and the base on which it is mounted if a one-piece mould is to be made. However, even simple hulls with no reverse curves or tapers are nowadays usually made in a two-piece mould, which makes it far easier to remove the mould from the plug and the hull from the mould. A wall of clay or Plasticine, or if the shape is suitable, a strip of ply is erected along the keel centre line and half the plug, including the wall, is treated with parting agent. This half is now laid up, running the glass up the wall, and when cured the wall removed, leaving a flange along the centre line. The rest of the plug and the flange are now treated and the second half laid up. When cured, holes are drilled through both flanges before moving the halves, so that they can be bolted together accurately.

Lay-up usually involves brushing on a gel coat, or the first coat of laminating resin if a gel coat is not used, and waiting for it to go tacky before placing glass mat in position and stippling through. A second layer of mat can be added, and even a third in the case of large, wide moulds, or strips of wood or wire etc, can be attached to the moulding to stiffen it. Overlaps should be teased out and tamped or stippled down thoroughly.

On removal from the plug (using gentle leverage with thin strips of wood to break the 'suction' if necessary) wash off the remnants of the parting film with water and inspect for flaws. Small ones can be filled with resin and rubbed and polished down, but it is better in the long run to try a new moulding if bad flaws exist. Polish the inside of the mould thoroughly.

Moulding a hull in the mould is similar – gel coat, mat or cloth, and plenty of stippling or rolling to squeeze out excess resin. Too much resin adds weight but little strength. Make sure that the glass is thoroughly wetted out and stippled firmly into corners, etc. Additional mat can be stippled down on areas requiring reinforcement. Remove from mould and trim while green, but replace in mould while curing takes place.

Internal fittings are best added while the resin is still very tacky, and can be reinforced by draping strips of cloth or mat over them and stippling down with more resin. Once cured, fittings are

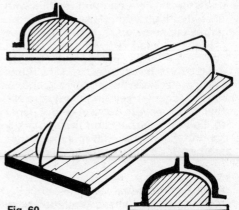

Fig. 60

best attached with epoxy glues, abrading the hull surface thoroughly (even down to the glass fibres) in the seating area to ensure a complete key.

Where weight of the finished hull is important, weigh out the resin and glass beforehand; you then know that you must distribute those quantities evenly to achieve the required result. Sport-type models are not usually critical on weight, nor are many scale models (if of reasonable size) but to produce

Left, three g.r.p. hulls, one monohedron with full-length spray rails, one 'warped bottom', and a hard-bilged round bilge design. Right, extensive vacuum forming in a small trawler kit.

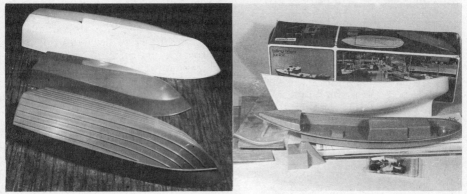

a strong and light competition hull with even distribution of glass and resin requires experience.

Hulls moulded with coloured gel coat can be polished with a good metal polish followed by car polish. For painting, wash the surface thoroughly to remove parting agent traces and any grease, then rub over with 400 wet-or-dry paper to cloud the surface and provide a key for the paint. Two-pot polyurethanes are best for a good and durable finish.

Polystyrene Hulls

Many kits nowadays include hulls vacuum-formed from polystyrene sheet, also loosely termed 'styrene' or just 'plastic', since the same sort of material sold in flat sheets is called 'plastic card'. There are actually a number of different plastics of similar general appearance but different strengths or other characteristics; for example, polystyrene will wrinkle if you paint on cellulose, but A.B.S. (the commonest alternative for hulls) will accept cellulose. All have in common the ability to soften when heated but return to former stiffness on cooling.

Vacuum forming is the best way of moulding sheets of these materials, a sheet being heated while positioned over a box containing a pattern or plug, then as it softens being lowered on to the plug while all the air in the box is quickly extracted. This requires a machine, of course, and although it is possible to build a small one the only practical approach to moulding an individual hull is to find a firm with a suitable size machine who will draw a hull for you from your solid wood or plaster plug.

However, plastic card can be used in the same way as thin ply or metal to build a hard chine hull, and it is particularly useful for superstructure construction, since it has no grain and crisp corners and edges are easily achieved. It is available in a considerable range of thicknesses from paper-thin up to ⅛in. (3mm) or more, but it is heavy, so care should be taken to use as thin a sheet as will do a particular job. Sawing and sanding should be kept to a minimum, as static electricity is rapidly generated and is a nuisance, attracting sawdust and general dirt. Cutting is best achieved by scoring the surface with a sharp knife-blade, when flexing the sheet will cause it to snap cleanly along the score. It is, however, glossy and slippery, and care is needed to keep control of the knife.

Adhesives may be in tube form (polystyrene cement) or a watery liquid (methyl ethyl ketone) which can be applied with a brush and which will work its own way along joints by capillary effect. Avoid excess adhesive – it works by dissolving the plastic and too much will create deformation. This, of course, applies equally to working on a vac-formed hull supplied in a kit. Bonding other materials to the plastic is not easy, though the adhesive used by plumbers for plastic pipework works reasonably well. Where possible an attachment should be held in place by straps or patches of plastic card; roughening of the surfaces to be joined is helpful.

Polystyrene is used for non-working plastic kits (aircraft, lorries, etc) and a range of sections for architectural modelling is available. For detail fittings (cranes, winches, davits, and the like) these sources are well worth examining.

Chapter Six

Superstructures

For the purposes of this chapter, a superstructure is any sizeable part of the boat from the deck up which requires constructional work. Fittings are dealt with in the next chapter.

A word or two on decks may not be amiss here. The best deck is undoubtedly cut from ply and fitted in one piece or such pieces as may be required where the foredeck and/or afterdeck occupy different levels. Ply decks can be convincingly marked (Chapter Nine), and it is not usually necessary to plank a deck unless the builder desires to do so, or unless a combination of extreme sheer and camber means that ply cannot be induced to take the curves.

The classic method of planking a deck is to fit a kingplank (often in a timber of contrasting colour) down the centre of the hull, its width being roughly ½in. for a 3ft. hull, and its thickness the same as that of the planking to be used. The two outside planks of the deck may be

of the same colour wood, about ¼in. wide, and a small sheet of the same timber can be fitted at the extreme bow and stern (Fig. 61), to provide a pleasing pattern. The planks themselves should be ⅜in. wide to fit in with the above example, and they are laid parallel with the outer hull line from the outside inwards. As each plank is cut, the end is shaped and laid over the king-plank, which is pared away to receive the plank ends (Fig. 62). This is known as 'joggling in'. When sanded smooth and varnished, a very attractive deck results.

A scale deck for a trawler, etc, will have the planks running straight fore and aft, but still requires the outer two planks to follow the shape of the hull (Fig. 63) to form the waterway. Where the deck is broken for a hatch, the planks terminate in a rebate on a plank laid athwartships, as in Fig. 64.

The built-up superstructure will normally be in the form of a cabin for a small boat, or a bridge and deckhouses,

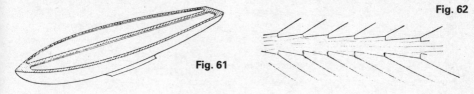

Fig. 62

Fig. 61

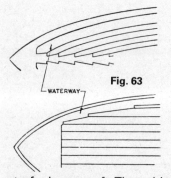

Fig. 63

WATERWAY

HATCH

Fig. 64

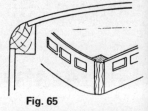

Fig. 65

etc, for larger craft. The golden rule is to keep all this 'top hamper' light in weight, and for maximum strength it is customary to make it in thin ply. Corners become rather difficult with thin materials, so corner-pieces of square timber are employed for reinforcement. Where a rounded corner exists, this is

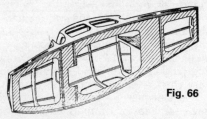

Fig. 66

shaped from a piece of timber of sufficient section to give the required radius, and the sides, etc, are rebated in (Fig. 65).

Many deck-houses and so forth have cambered roofs, and these are usually set up on ply frames cut to give the required camber. The frames are fretted

out to save weight, and must be positioned between any ports or windows. Fig. 66 shows a typical cabin structure made in this way. Curved fronts, etc, require horizontal formers, and should be cut so that the natural bend of the ply helps assembly. All ply-to-ply joints should be made with the aid of a fillet strip which need be no more than ⅛in. square (Fig. 67).

Metal such as thin aluminium or tinplate can be used for superstructures, using riveted or soldered joints, but little advantage is gained, and unless a considerable saving in weight can be effected there is little point in using such materials, although in the case of steam models metal will, of course, tolerate heat which would warp a wooden structure.

Frequently, the cabin or other superstructure is removable to allow access to the interior, and it must therefore be strong enough to withstand a certain amount of handling. The joint around the base should be watertight, since few models avoid splashes on the deck during operation, and a fast boat in particular produces spray which, while it may be thrown clear in calm weather,

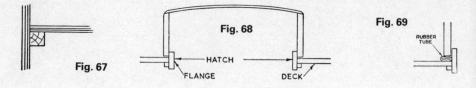

Fig. 67

Fig. 68

HATCH

FLANGE

DECK

Fig. 69

RUBBER TUBE

44

is often blown over the boat in a breeze. To prevent water seeping in, a flange, called a coaming, can be fitted to the deck all round each hatch, over which the superstructure fits (Fig. 68). Additional protection can be given to a non-scale boat by fitting a soft, thin-walled rubber tube outside this flange, the superstructure being clipped down in such a way as to squash the tube and provide an excellent seal.

The plain coaming round the aperture will usually prove sufficient to retain the superstructure in place; alternatively, dowels can be mounted in small blocks glued in each corner of the unit, plugging into corresponding holes in blocks glued in the hatch. When a positive, quick-action clip is desired, mount Terry clips at each end (or in each corner) of the superstructure and provide spigots to engage them in the hull itself (Fig. 70). Springs or rubber bands are sometimes used (Fig. 71), but take longer to hook up. Magnets may be used.

Hatches may also be fitted and sealed in the above ways, except where a flush hatch is needed. This often arises when the superstructure is too small to provide adequate access, and it is therefore secured to the deck and a portion of the deck made to lift out. Fig. 72 shows a suitable seal for this type of joint.

As an alternative to removable cabins, etc, some boats have only the cabin top removable. This means that the structure offers no sealing difficulty around its base, and the chance of water entering is lessened by the extra inch or two of height, and also the fact that most tops will overhang the sides, front, etc, i.e. there is no corner to collect the water. A simple plug-in top is therefore satisfactory (Fig. 73).

When a considerable amount of equipment is carried, or access is otherwise required on a large scale (as with some steam plants) most of the deck is made detachable. In this case the inwales are better if slightly more generous, and strip of rubber (aircraft type, or cut from a cycle inner tube) or a strip of draught-sealing foam can be cemented in place to form a water seal. Quick release fittings can be made by solder-

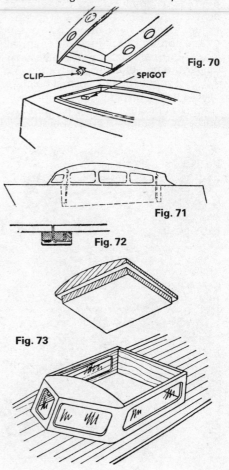

CLIP   SPIGOT   Fig. 70

Fig. 71

Fig. 72

Fig. 73

Fig. 74

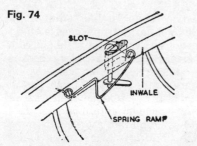

ing tags on small screws, the tags passing through slots in the inwales and tightening the deck down by running over a sprung ramp fitted to the inwale (Fig. 74). Such decks are usually inset below the hull planking, of course (Fig. 42), and should have a normal hatch for access to the motor.

Most superstructures are fitted with ports or windows, ports being used where there is a chance of volumes of water breaking over. Ports are as a rule flush with the external surface, i.e. they do not have a projecting rim, although with small boats a brass flange may be visible. The best representation is simply a cleanly cut hole with celluloid behind it, but this is unsatisfactory if the material thickness is greater than about 1/16in. With thick material, it is best to drill the hole slightly oversize and cement in a seamless curtain ring or a thin slice cut from a brass tube flush with the surface. This forms a rebate against which a disc of celluloid may be cemented. If the porthole has been cut out with a sharpened brass tube (sharpened inside, not outside) and the same tube used for the 'glass' and rebate, everything should be a tidy fit.

Windows, on the other hand, usually have a slightly raised frame or a bead on their outer faces, and are unlikely to be cut in anything thicker than 1/8in. ply. To produce the raised frame, cut a blank from bristol board, veneer, or 1/32in. ply, to the outside shape, and cement accurately in place. Mark out the actual window and fret out. Alternatively, bend a bead from florists' or similar wire, and cement in place, or varnish a length of thread or fishing line, allow to dry drawn taut, and form the bead from the resulting stiffened thread, cemented in place. The celluloid is cemented behind the window. Another method is to sandwich a piece of clear plastic cut to the outside shape of the frame between the cut frame and the cut-out in the superstructure, which makes the clear pane very secure.

Most of the deck and superstructure detaches for access to the steam plant of this straight-running torpedo boat destroyer.

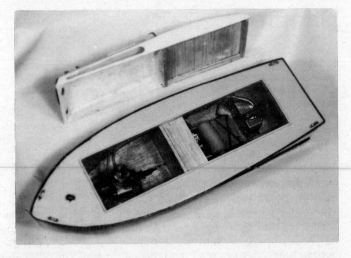

A simple but fast two-shelf design by the author with a one-piece removable superstructure. Roomy interior belies the fact that the model is only 20ins. long.

For such purposes, celluloid or clear acetate sheeting can be used. It pays to use these materials in a thickness of at least ·010in. and the shapes can be cut by merely scratching the surface and cracking the shape out. Coins and washers of various sizes help to cut true circles, but if you are building a liner model it is well worth making or investing in a punch for cutting accurate port glasses. If the celluloid or acetate is cemented in place *before* painting, scraps of paper can be stuck in place with soap to mask the glazing off during painting. A line of cabin windows can be glazed after painting if required, by using one long strip of celluloid held in place by $1/16$in. $\times 1/8$in. strips pinned along its edges. Ports can be simulated by pinning a sheet of plastic behind them and pouring clear casting resin into each port, removing the plastic backing when the resin has set.

Internal combustion engines need to draw in a fair quantity of air, and it is often convenient to arrange half open windows and skylights to allow for this breathing.

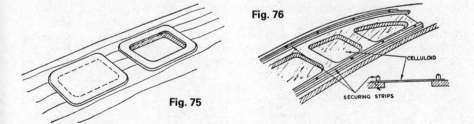

Fig. 75

Fig. 76

CELLULOID

SECURING STRIPS

Chapter Seven

Fittings

The question of fittings for the average semi-scale launch type of model is one that is entirely up to the individual builder. Near-scale models must have a certain minimum of detail, and this can be patterned after that used for scale boats. Yacht fittings are in a separate class, of course, and are dealt with in another chapter. Certain items are found under different guises in various forms of models, and it will therefore be advisable if we work through the various fittings from the simplest to the advanced. As with the superstructure, light weight for all fittings is essential.

Launch types usually have a mooring post and a pair of towing posts, fairleads to suit, handrails, a ventilator or two usually of the airscoop type, and possibly steaming and riding lights and a syren. The posts are easily made from pieces of square timber with a drilled hole in which is driven a stub of brass wire (Fig. 78). All edges are bevelled, and cuts are taken out of the four

corners below the wire to produce a waisted effect. In full scale, the posts run down to main hull members, so if they are mounted in the corners of a well, their full length must be shown.

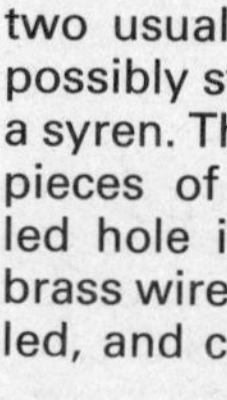

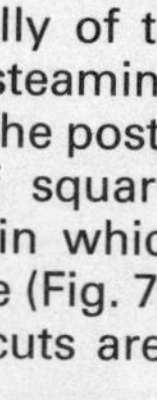

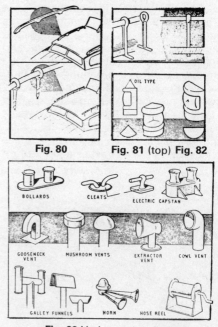

Fig. 80   **Fig. 81** (top) **Fig. 82**

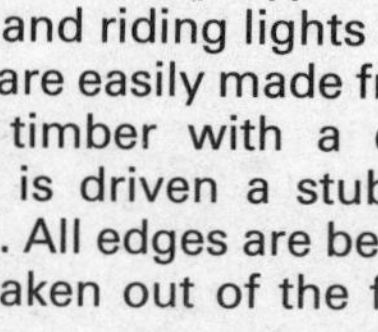

Fig. 83 Various other fittings.

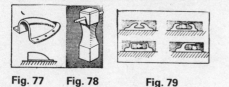

Fig. 77   **Fig. 78**   **Fig. 79**

Fairleads are merely guides to contain a rope, and on small craft look like the top left example in Fig. 79. They can be carved from a close-grained wood such as box, or cut from plastic or metal sheet.

Handrails or grabrails on small boats are frequently cut from a length of timber as in Fig. 80, and are fitted directly to cabin tops, etc. Alternatively, they may be made by screwing in 000 brass screw-eyes, sliding through a length of brass wire, and soldering. Welding or brazing rod is the best brass wire, since it is hard-drawn (stiff) and usually dead straight. A further variation is to use split pins as the stanchions, especially where a screw-eye offers insufficient length (Fig. 81).

Airscoop vents are difficult to fabricate, although not all that hard to carve from timber. A fairly easy system is to mould them from thick acetate sheet, carving a male mould and a matching hole in a small piece of ply. Soften the acetate by laying it over the mould in a warm oven (about 230°F is average softening point), then push the piece of ply over until fully home. Remove the moulding, cut the vent opening, and trim the base to shape. (Fig. 77)

Steaming and riding lights are usually quarter-round and half-round (Fig. 82), and may be carved from dowel or fabricated from scraps of wood or plastic. Coloured plastic beads (sold for children) can be cut to provide the lenses.

Syrens may be single or paired, and for small craft resemble modern motorcar external horns. The mechanism end offers little problem, but the bell is delicate and is best shaped from something like a plastic golf tee. The modeller making his own details soon acquires a stock of old toothbrush handles, knitting needles, electrical parts, and suchlike odds and ends, which, when raked over, frequently offer the solution to minor problems!

Larger boats than those so far begin to sport such things as bollards, cleats, cowl vents, chain, rails, skylights, ships' wheels, etc. Bollards can be produced in wood, using dowel and thin ply discs on a ply base, or in metal, when the easiest way is to use brass screws or rivets, filed off flat on top and cut off to length, soldered to a brass base-plate. Cleats are metal versions of mooring posts on a smaller scale, and are simply made from split pins with soldered brass wires and washers.

Cowl vents are another ticklish proposition – they never look satisfactory carved from wood, and small hollow balls which can be halved and cemented to dowels are not easily come by. The ends of some small cigar tubes or pill containers, etc., can be cut off and used, but the easiest way is to mould the cowls from acetate sheet. A hemispheric mould (the end of a small test tube, for example), and a suitable hole drilled in a piece of ply are the simplest requirements; the acetate is cut into squares, softened (230°F), and each cowl is individually formed by pushing through the hole with the mould. For mass production, lay various-sized ball bearings on a metal tray and pop in a low oven. Lay the acetate over the bearings and warm, when it will drop over the balls. This can

Fig. 84 Moulding cowl vents.

Assorted cowl vents. Note handles on left-hand examples and rotation joints on all. Each is accurate to a prototype.

be aided by light pressure with a soft foam rubber sponge. Carefully trim the resulting hemispheres and cement them to appropriate diameter dowels trimmed to a suitable angle and length.

Chain is best purchased, but if you wish to make it, it can be done by winding phosphor-bronze or brass wire tightly on another wire of a diameter corresponding to the link size required. A long cut is then made with a fine saw or knife-edge file along one side of the coil, so that the turns are all severed, and may be slid off as cut links. They are then fitted together and each one is soldered (place solder paste on each and pass through a flame), after which a narrow wire is slipped into each in turn and the links squeezed to ovality with pliers.

Rails are a problem in that stanchions need to be turned for perfect results.

However, long fine split pins can be modified with patience (Fig. 85), or the rail can be laid out on a block, the longitudinals passed through the plain split pins, and the gaps in the sides of the pins filled with solder. The top rail can be brass wire and the lower ones stranded cable (wire ropes are customary on smallish vessels). The only suitable cable is 'Laystrate' wire sold for control-line model aircraft, and not too much paint must be used or the effect of the stranded wire will be lost.

Skylights are relatively simple if built up from thin ply as in Fig. 86. If it is desired to hinge the frames, this is best done by means of a strip of silk or plastic drawing film glued in place. Frosted glass may be simulated by rubbing the acetate with fine glasspaper, two good strokes at 90° being best. The safety bars stand proud of the frames and should be made from copper wire, the ends being pinched to flatten them.

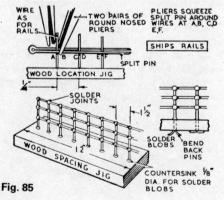

Fig. 85

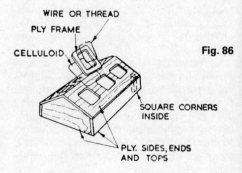

Fig. 86

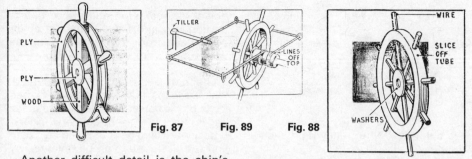

Fig. 87   **Fig. 89**   **Fig. 88**

Another difficult detail is the ship's wheel. In fairly large scale (1½in. diameter or so) it is quite possible to make a wheel from thin ply discs and rings, with square spokes shaped only outside the outer ring (Fig. 87). Smaller wheels are easier in metal, and are best produced by drilling a tube for spokes and slicing off the drilled portion. The wire spokes are slipped through and soldered to a central washer, a second washer being soldered on the other side (Fig. 88). A few minutes with a needle file will shape the wire ends.

A working wheel can be constructed by adding a double pulley (made from washers) to the shaft, and winding on three or four turns of twine from each direction. The twine is led out athwartship, turned through smooth wire loops and taken aft, turned again and made off on the tiller. Spinning the wheel either way will produce the correct rudder action only if the lines come off the *top* of the pulley (Fig. 89).

Lifebelts can be made from several things, fat curtain rings (especially bone and wood), being excellent. Alternatives are small rubber tyres, O-rings, fishing rod rings, and similar items. Lifebelts normally have a line round them, secured to the belt by four equal-spaced whippings (Fig. 90) of about eight turns. It is quite sufficient to cement the ends of the whippings, which

makes a neat job; the method of producing blind ends is shown in Fig. 91, and may be used if preferred. A little trouble in finding a thread or twine with a pronounced twist is well worthwhile – it looks so much more like scale rope.

Masts are made from timber as a rule, with birch dowel being widely used. Tapering is a rather tedious business, but may be hastened by planing the dowel on four sides before applying glasspaper. Mast caps (Fig. 92) can be cut from thin ply or thick celluloid. Metal tube can be used for masts, particularly if salvaged from lightweight tapered or telescopic aerials; light weight is still an essential requirement. Step masts in blocks screwed to bulkheads, or pass them through the deck right down to a step screwed to the keelson. If a mast is fitted to a detachable unit, it should extend through to the bottom of

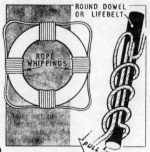

Fig. 90   **Fig. 91**

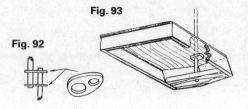

Fig. 92

Fig. 93

the unit (Fig. 93) for really rigid anchorage.

Rigging is always rather a nuisance, since nine times out of ten it will interfere with the removal of part of the superstructure. One way round is to use shirring elastic where possible, providing a small hook to engage an eye at the foot of the stay or shroud. Where three or four shrouds make off close together, they can be made off to a wire engaging in clips on the bulwark, etc. Another way is to terminate each line in a tiny coil spring which, while only comprising three or four turns, is enough to tension the rigging. Permanent rigging can be made from 'Laystrate' wire and tiny split pins represent deck eyes, etc very well.

Most boats employ at least a few rigging blocks, the most frequent types being stropped blocks and sheaved blocks. Stropped blocks can be made from dowel with the aid of needle files (Fig. 94), and are more or less permanent fixtures. Sheaved blocks include a pulley, and may be single, double, or treble. The pulley can be filed from

dowel or plastic rod and drilled before parting off, and fitted with a strap or case made from thin brass or tinplate with a tiny wire eye soldered on (Fig. 95).

Lifeboats are usually stowed covered, which means that they can be carved from block balsa. Most early lifeboats, and many on present-day small workboats, were clincher built, and an excellent representation can be obtained by carving the hull slightly undersize and glueing on paper planks – rather a fiddly business, but producing an excellent result. The canvas covers should be added after, from bristol board or ply, covered with part of an old handkerchief, since it is not easy to carve the tops flat enough to be convincing. Boats stowed without covers are usually secured inverted, again obviating the need to hollow the hull. Cheap toy plastic boats are frequently suitable for dinghies, etc, after slight modifications, but if you wish to make your own boats completely, they can be made in the same way as larger models, or carved from the solid (lime or obeche give good results) with the aid of lino-cutting gouges.

Rolled gummed paper is perfectly satisfactory for funnels, though for a more scale-like thickness brass shim with a soldered seam is preferable. Tinplate is often used, and the funnel

Fig. 94

Fig. 95

STAY
EYES

Fig. 96

Fig. 97

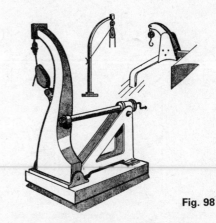

Fig. 98

bands are also of brass or tinplate cut into narrow strips, or wire soldered into place. Steam pipes and syrens can be fabricated quite simply from thin-walled brass tube, or, if bends are required, copper tube.

Anchors can be made up from the scrap box, copper being extremely useful since it works easily. The two most common patterns are shown in Fig. 97.

Davits can be formed from brass wire, suitably tapered, or, if of the Columbus or similar pattern (Fig. 98), cut from ply and brought to the required width with wood fairings. A drilled hole or a stub of brass tube held in place with a silk patch will provde a pivot if the davits are to be fully working.

A small jig should be constructed for the assembly of ladders (Fig. 99). Metal ladders are a straightforward soldering job in wire, and wood-type ones can be made in ply or in soldered brass shim.

The building of winches, capstans, windlasses and so on is greatly aided by an assortment of old clock parts, cotton reels, electrical coil bobbins, and the like. In these, as with other detail, photographs of full-size gear are of considerable assistance in obtaining an authentic appearance.

The rudder is an important part of any model, and is usually cut from brass sheet and soldered in a saw-cut in a length of brass rod. The rod passes

through a bush in the hull (Fig. 100), or through a tube located by soldered washers (Fig. 101). It is important that the top of the bush or tube is well above the waterline to prevent leaks. Thick paint should be flowed into the bottom assembly with a screwed bush, for the same purpose; with soldered washers, the bottom should be soldered first, then paint flowed round and the top washer slipped in place. Rivet the end of the tube over, to draw the bottom up tight, before soldering.

Rudder shape is only important in high speed radio models; beginners and simple models need only worry about movement (25-30° each side) and area, though it is hard to give a general rule for area. About 1¼ sq. in per foot of hull length is a rough guide. It is cus-

Fig. 99

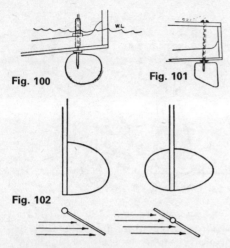

Fig. 100

Fig. 101

Fig. 102

describing various detail fittings, but most of the common ones have been touched on above. In addition to materials so far mentioned, the scale builder will find Paxolin tube extremely useful; it is available in sizes of from ⅛in. up to 2½in. diameter, is light in weight, and can be cemented. For torpedo tubes, circular hatches, small gun turrets and barbettes, and all other parts calling for largish tubing, it is invaluable. Flat or one-way curved structures can be constructed from plastic card (polystyrene sheet) which can also be heat-formed into more complex shapes. Small repetitive details requiring crisp outlines can be cast in low-temperature metal (see model soldier materials) or cast-

tomary nowadays to balance the rudder (Fig. 102) to reduce the force required to turn it, except on full-keel or scale models (Fig. 103), although even this type of rudder can be partially balanced, as shown in the sketch.

A friction adjustment is necessary if no radio is fitted and the boat will be free-running, and this can be cut and bent up from brass (Fig. 104). An alternative, where the tiller is not required, is to thread the rudder stock to receive nuts and a washer (or solder a washer in place) compressing a short coil spring which in effect jams the rudder at the bottom. The adjusting knob can frequently be disguised as an item of ship's gear.

A complete book could be written in

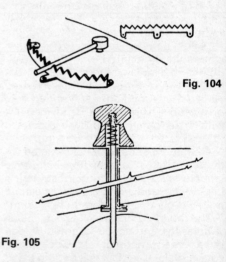

Fig. 104

Fig. 105

ing resin in silicon rubber moulds produced from patterns made from wood, plastic, metal, etc.

Naturally, most ship fittings can be purchased ready-made and can give a very professional-looking air to a model. Many modellers, however, derive great satisfaction from using their ing-

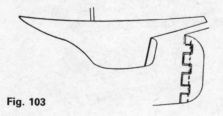

Fig. 103

East European model of a Russian survey ship, about 4ft. long, gives an indication of the quantity and delicacy of detail in top-level working competition models.

enuity to reproduce detail, and it is surprising what everyday things can be pressed into service. Cut-off pygmy light bulbs or ground-off wine glasses make excellent turrets for air/sea rescue launches, old torch reflectors are excellent for certain types of radar scanner, sections of combs provide fiddly gratings, and so on; a little imagination to 'see' the final result is all that is needed.

Do look at actual boats — or at least photos — of similar type to that which you are building. Decide on the approximate scale of your model and cut out a rough human figure to that scale, from thin card. Use it to check door heights, lifebelt and wheel diameters, etc. The commonest fault with freelance scale-type models is inconsistency of scale.

Chapter Eight

Yacht Fittings

The fittings required for a model yacht differ in that they are strictly functional. Generally speaking, much the same fittings are required whatever the yacht, although naturally the bigger the model the stronger the fittings must be.

In constructing a 'traditional' or scale form hull we would have made the complete fin up in wood. This must now be cut to provide the pattern for casting the lead, and the cut piece must be thoroughly painted or shellacked, and smoothed to a good finish. Now make two rough boxes a little larger than the pattern, open on one face, and matching fairly well when the open faces are together. Drill the top of the pattern and insert two dowels spaced so that they exactly fit the keel bolt holes, and cut the boxes to allow the dowels to protrude through one side. Wax polish the pattern and dowels. Now mix sufficent plaster of paris to fill one of the boxes, making it slightly on the runny side. Fill the box and place the pattern on to the wet plaster, pushing down until it is exactly half submerged. Check that the dowels are in position, and hold for a few seconds until the plaster has set.

Drill small holes in three corners of the back of the second box, and a larger hole in the other corner. Shellac the face of the set plaster and grease lightly, then place the second box in position and pour in plaster until overflowing. Allow to set, then gently separate the boxes and remove the pattern. Chase out the plaster to make a filling hole (Fig. 107) and at the highest point of the mould a breather hole. Bake the two moulds or allow to dry out thoroughly for a few days.

Bend two lengths of studding to form 'hockey-sticks', and lay them in place in

Fig. 106

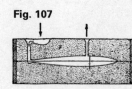

Fig. 107

Fig. 108

the holes formed by the dowels. Slip nuts on to prevent them sliding too far in, and check that adequate thread projects for passing up into the boat. Now strap the boxes together firmly and stand between a couple of bricks, or similar. Cut into small pieces slightly more lead than will be needed for the finished casting, and melt down in an old saucepan or paint kettle. Pour smoothly in a thin stream into the filling hole until visible in the breather hole; fill to the top and allow to cool. When cold, separate the mould halves and check the casting for flaws. Cut off the two cores and remove any flash; check weight and truth. Clean up with a worn file and old emery. Flat faces can be planed with an ordinary plane if lubricated with turpentine.

Fit the lead accurately to the deadwood (the remainder of the fin) which must, of course, be drilled for the bolts.

The heel of the lead, if of the usual pattern, must be located with the deadwood, which is best done by sawing a slit and inserting a slip of brass or similar, retaining this in place with epoxy or copper rivets through lead and timber. Before permanently assembling, varnish the timber faces two or three coats, and varnish the lead faces immediately before clamping together. Any discrepancy arising through cleaning up or reducing weight should be made up with a slip of timber between the lead and the wood during assembly.

Bulb keels can be cast in two halves (left and right if asymmetric), but with modern fins are usually one-piece castings with a slot cast in to slip over the fin. Symmetrical torpedo or teardrop shapes can use a wood pattern turned on a lathe or hand carved from bread and butter block. The mould boxes are similar but require a piece of the fin

material accurately secured in place to cast the slot in; it can be sawn in the cast lead but it is laborious work.

It is quite possible to laminate a lead from sheet lead, provided it is scoured with glass-paper before epoxying the laminations together. Brass or stainless rods or screws can later be inserted as an extra precaution. An alternative is to mould the bulb in glass-fibre and fill the resulting shell with slivers of lead or shot. This means a slightly larger bulb, as the lead cannot be compacted to the same extent as a casting, but for many yachts the difference is insignificant in terms of performance. It is also possible to buy ready-cast lead bulbs in different weights.

If casting, always make sure that everything is bone dry. Moisture in a mould or on the lead dropped into the melt will turn explosively into steam, spraying molten lead around, while the presence of grease or wax in the mould can give rise to accidents which may be imagined.

Radio yachts almost without exception use a spade rudder, which is a balanced, wholly pivoted surface requiring only a bush through the hull. The rudder stock needs to be strong — bending forces are considerable — and usually extends about a third of the depth into the rudder blade, which is often two laminations of timber with the grains slightly crossed to prevent warping. The pivot line should allow

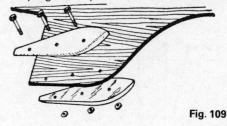

Fig. 109

57

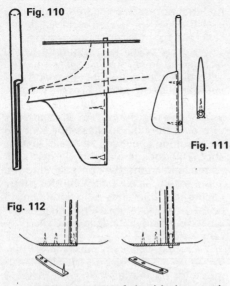

Fig. 110

Fig. 111

Fig. 112

about 25 per cent of the blade area in front. Most vane (and non-racing radio) yachts employ a skeg as described in Chapter Four; this was built in and must now be fitted with the rudder trunk. This is a length of brass tube extending from slightly above deck level to the bottom of the skeg; where it emerges from the canoe body the rear half of the tube is removed by sawing (Fig. 110). The rear of the skeg should be channelled to receive the tube, and the tube posi-tioned after varnishing or painting the channel. Small pins may be used to secure the cut-away part of the tube, but the heads must be filed away to leave a smooth bearing for the rudder stock.

The stock is a length of tube fitting snugly in the trunk, and the rudder is screwed to it (Fig. 111), the screwheads being filed away afterwards. A small plate screwed to the bottom of the skeg makes the lower bearing, either by hav-ing a pintle soldered in, engaging the stock, or being drilled to receive a pin fitted in the stock (Fig. 112). At the upper end, the stock must be long enough to provide fixing for the Braine quadrant or vane tiller; the best means of doing this is to sweat a threaded plug in the tube or use a pinch-bolt.

A similar rudder arrangement may be employed for a full-keel boat (Fig. 113), but in the model world this type of keel is not frequently encountered except in the EC12 one-design class.

Inside the hull there is usually only one fitting, the mast step, although many radio yachts use a deck-stepped mast and can thus seal off the hull except for the radio installation. A through-deck mast is a little more com-plex but provides more control over mast curvature and hence sail setting.

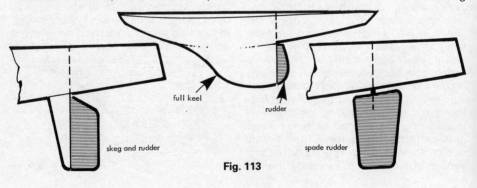

full keel

rudder

skeg and rudder

spade rudder

Fig. 113

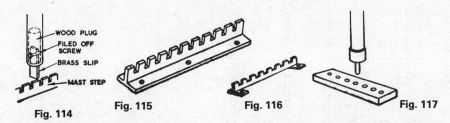

WOOD PLUG
FILED OFF SCREW
BRASS SLIP
MAST STEP

Fig. 114 **Fig. 115** **Fig. 116** **Fig. 117**

The mast is always adjustable fore and aft and in rake in order to trim the yacht for the best possible performance; some skippers fix its position after trimming and seal off the deck, but others retain the capability of adjustment in case of future sail changes, etc. Some radio skippers use a larger tube up to main boom level, into which different mast/sail combinations can be plugged, though this is not allowed in all classes. In all cases the mast step provides part of the adjustment.

The heel of the mast is fitted with a tongue which engages one of several slots in the step (Fig. 114) to choice. For smaller yachts, the step can be cut from part of a piece of brass curtain rail (Fig. 115), but for larger boats it is built up from a strip of heavy-gauge brass to which are silver-soldered feet (Fig. 116). The step is screwed directly to the backbone.

The mast slide is the second adjustment on the mast position and rake, and consists of a plate sliding in a tray (Fig. 118). A ferrule hard soldered to the plate accepts the mast, and holes are provided in both plate and tray to receive a pin, locking the plate in position. The tray is screwed in place on the deck, beams being positioned beneath, and a slot is cut in the deck to correspond with the slot in the tray.

Deck-stepped masts may use a similar mast tongue and T-shaped step, or may use a step which is a series of drilled holes in a metal, plastic or even ply plate (Fig. 117). The mast heel is either plugged and a screw or cup-hook inserted and sawn off to form a peg fitting the holes, or a moulded nylon peg fitting can be used.

Most masts nowadays are untapered aluminimum alloy tube (3/8 or 1/2in. for 36R, 1/2 or 5/8in. for M, 5/8 or 3/4in. for 10r and 3/4in. or larger for A) although carbon fibre or specially drawn aluminium grooved masts can be bought. Wood is infrequent except for small models.

Rigging tends to be very simple, often a stainless steel wire shroud each side plus a backstay and forestay, using a masthead jumper strut for the fore and aft stays (Fig. 119). Sometimes a single-spreader strut and diamond stay is used, the spreader being epoxied through the mast and bent fore or aft to push the mast into a slight curve. Wires are made off into the eyes of heavier gauge wire hooks, which can be of V-form to hook into holes drilled in the mast tube or S-form to engage eyes or holes drilled in sheet metal. Wire rigging is tensioned with bottle-screws or

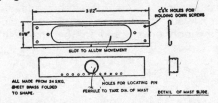

3 1/2"

C'S'K HOLES FOR HOLDING DOWN SCREWS

SLOT TO ALLOW MOVEMENT

1 1/8"

ALL MADE FROM 24 S.W.G.
SHEET BRASS FOLDED
TO SHAPE.

HOLES FOR LOCATING PIN

FERRULE TO TAKE DIA. OF MAST

DETAIL OF MAST SLIDE.

Fig. 118 Dimensions for a 10R yacht.

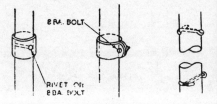

Fig. 121   Fig. 122   Fig. 123

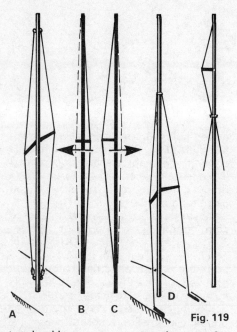

turnbuckles, or sometimes for backstays on small models a short cord is introduced with bowsie adjustment. All-cord rigging (braided terylene fishing line is best) is adequately adjusted with bowsies (Fig. 120). Some builders prefer to silver-solder eyes and other fittings to mast bands which slip over the mast snugly and can be held in place by a single bolt right through (Fig. 121) or clamped with a small bolt (Fig. 122).

A jackline is usually fitted down the after side of the mast; this again is stainless steel wire, and is passed through eyes fitted to the mast and

Fig. 120 Left to right, wire flat and circular bowsies, turnbuckle, and bottle screw.

soldered to a screw or bolt top and bottom. It must be really taut. The eyes can be small screw-eyes with a wood mast, or split pins for a metal mast, fitted as Fig. 123.

Alternatively, the jackline can be threaded in and out of pairs of holes drilled every few inches up the mast, or simply secured top and bottom and held to the mast at intervals with plastic insulation tape. Where a pocket luff sail, or one secured by mast rings or cord, is used no jackline is necessary.

Booms are frequently of smaller diameter alloy tube or sometimes of very light I section alloy, but many yachts use wood booms planed to a taper (Fig. 124) with brass shim bands wrapped and soldered at points of attachment for eyes, etc to prevent splitting or pulling out of the eyes. The mainboom is attached to the mast by a gooseneck (Fig. 125 is an example) which allows the boom to swivel freely from side to

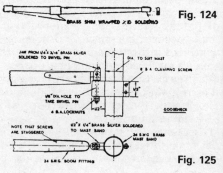

Fig. 124

Fig. 125

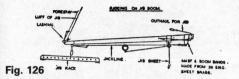

Fig. 126

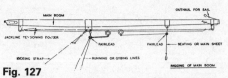

Fig. 127

side and, by a horizontal pivot, the outer end to rise and fall.

The jib is frequently permanently bent to its boom, so that separate booms are required for each suit of sails. Figs. 126 and 127 show a typical rigging set-up for both booms for a sophisticated free-sailing yacht. The two types of bowsie (or bowser) used, with the correct methods of reeving them, are shown in Fig. 128.

When a boat is sailing, the wind pressure tends to belly the sail and lift the boom. For running this is acceptable, since it cushions gusts which might otherwise cause the boat to gybe or broach. On other courses, however, it is a disadvantage and a kicking strap is therefore fitted to hold the boom down.

This may be strong rigging line with bowsie adjustment on small models (Fig. 129) but wire with bottle-screw adjustment is normal for yachts over 36in. It must swivel freely with the boom. A similar strap may be fitted to the jib, but many boats achieve tensioning of the leach by siting the boom pivot two or three inches aft and pulling up on the boom fore end with the jibstay or forestay. Kicking straps are eased as the wind falls and hardened as it rises.

The remaining deck fittings consists of a jib rack (there are many forms of jib fitting, of varying complexity, but a simple rack is commonplace), two chainplates (or shroud plates) and sundry eyes depending on the form of sail sheeting and steering method. The jib-rack is often from T-section brass with a

row of holes (Fig. 130) giving adjustment for the jib boom swivel hook, which may be a simple S hook or incorporate a fishing swivel; this fitting takes a fair load and must be secure. Chain-

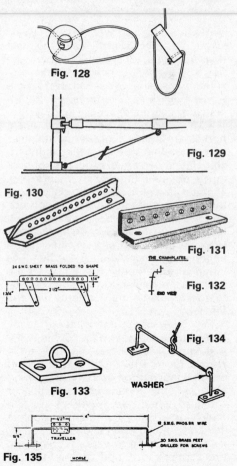

Fig. 128

Fig. 129

Fig. 130

Fig. 131

Fig. 132

Fig. 134

Fig. 133

Fig. 135

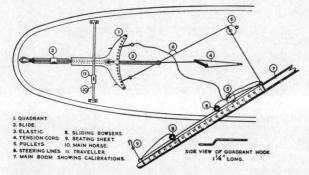

Fig. 136 Diagrammatic arangement of Braine gear in its basic form.

1. QUADRANT.
2. SLIDE.
3. ELASTIC.
4. TENSION CORD.
5. PULLEYS.
6. STEERING LINES.
7. MAIN BOOM SHOWING CALIBRATIONS.
8. SLIDING BOWSERS.
9. BEATING SHEET.
10. MAIN HORSE.
11. TRAVELLER.

SIDE VIEW OF QUADRANT HOOK
1 ¼" LONG.

plates may be screwed to the inwale through the deck slightly aft of the mast (Fig. 131 type) or extended down the hull side (fig. 132) since these take considerable strain. Eyes can be simple screw-eyes (insert, remove, epoxy, replace) or eye plates as in Fig. 133.

Many non-radio yachts use sheet horses from stout brass or stainless wire, the sheet hooks sliding athwartship directly on small models or engaging a traveller fitted with rollers (Fig. 135) on larger models. Stops prevent the hook or roller fouling at the corners, and these stops can be adjustable collars with grub screws, to limit hook travel or set up for a greater boom angle on one tack than the other. The latter arrangement can be used on radio yachts having rudder control only, to make sailing more interesting and efficient.

Two types of automatic steering may be seen. Braine gear (Fig. 136) is really obsolete but sometimes encountered in simple form. The yacht is trimmed to sail to windward on sail trim alone, and the gear only engaged for reaching or running, when the quadrant tension and hook position is balanced against sail pull. The jib is set slightly in so that if the yacht turns towards the wind jib pressure will turn it off again; if it turns away from the wind increased mainsail pressure will move the quadrant and return the boat to its required course. This is just the principle and there is much more to getting maximum control; probably the most easily available information appeared in *Model Boats* magazine for June 1983.

Vane gear works on the principle that a vane feather edge-on to the wind produces no force, but if one side or other is turned to the wind (by the boat turning) it will be blown back to edge-on. If the feather is linked to the rudder the feather movement will be translated to rudder movement, turning the boat until the feather and rudder are once more at 'neutral' and the boat back on its set course – in relation to the wind. If the wind changes direction, so will the yacht.

To sail different courses it must be possible to set the feather, and it is therefore frictionally mounted on a spindle so that it can be turned by hand but it will not move on the spindle

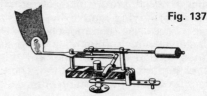

Fig. 137

Fig. 138 A simple vane gear, suitable for Marbleheads, etc. A. Main Body (channel brass ¼in. square). B. End Bearings (⅛in. i.d. brass tube). C. Compensation Arm (brass rod ¹/₁₆in. dia. threaded for weight – H). D. Vane Arm (brass strip ¹/₁₆in. × ⅜in.). E. Quadrant ¹/₃₂in. brass with 6BA nut soldered each end to take 6BA bolts for adjusting length of tack. F. Main Quadrant (¹/₁₆in. brass drilled ¹/₁₆in. holes). G. Aluminium Discs (2 off for supporting vane with 6BA bolt passing through). H. Lead Weight, threaded for adjustment. I. J. Brass spindles for vane arm and compensating

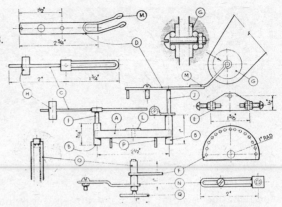

arm (⅛in. brass). K. Brass Pin ¹/₁₆in. diameter to engage compensating arm C when self-tacking. L. Brass Plate soldered on top of open channel and drilled to take tube O. M. Brass Rod ¹/₁₆in. diameter soldered to D and doubled to take vane. N. Vane Tiller ¹/₁₆in. brass doubled and soldered to tube O. 6BA bolt and nut fitted in gap and movable. O. Main Vane Bearing – brass tube with stub of ⅛in. rod soldered in top. Main spindle of ⅛in. brass fits in tube – top of spindle pointed to make needle bearing. P. Two ¹/₁₆in. Brass Pins to engage in holes in main quadrant F. Q. Main Base of ⅛in. brass with main spindle threaded and soldered on.

under the influence of the wind. The spindle is mounted on a pivot and the tiller connecting arm is firmly fixed to the spindle. Thus the yacht can be held pointing in the desired direction, the rudder held central and the feather arm turned to line up with the wind.

However, if the feather is set to sail the yacht to windward, it will only operate on one tack, and to sail into wind up a lake requires the yacht to change tack, or to zig-zag from bank to bank. In racing it would be necessary to stop the yacht and reset the vane at the end of each leg, so a self-tacking mechanism is incorporated, and it is this which gives the average vane gear its apparent complexity.

For reaching and running the gear is 'locked' and behaves as our simple friction vane described. For beating the mechanism is unlocked, and the vane arm is then free to move some 45° or so

either side of centre. This movement is limited by adjustable stops, and it will be clear that the feather can only exert pressure on the rudder when the arm is up against one of the stops. The yacht is trimmed so that there is a tendency to come up into wind and the slight one-way pressure of the vane against the stop controls this. When put about the same function is repeated on the opposite tack. The vane arm needs to move (usually) around 30° either side of centre and is finely adjustable to enable the yacht to achieve maximum performance.

This self-tacking function can be used for guying, where the yacht can be put off and will change tack and sail back to the same bank after a predetermined distance. This is done with a simple rubber band, the tension in the band and the angle through which it is applied being the main factors in when the

tack change occurs. The vane arm is merely biased by the rubber to the opposite tack, and all the while the yacht is sailing its proper course will have no effect. However, no wind or wave conditions are stable, and as soon as the yacht heads fractionally towards the wind or heels at a lesser angle, the band will snap the vane over and the yacht will change tack. Reading wind, water and rubber correctly to achieve a guy at exactly the right time or distance takes skill and experience, but it is highly satisfying and can win a race.

Other points in vane setting worth mentioning are that as experience grows the vane is set for an 'apparent wind', not the true wind (the apparent wind is the resultant of the true wind and the wind of the yacht's own motion), that the ratio between the lengths of the vane actuating arm and the tiller should be adjustable (about half the vane angular movement is normal on the rudder, but it can vary) and, because the force generated by the wind on the feather is very small, everything must be smooth, friction-free and carefully balanced.

Visiting clubs and talking to members it the finest way to learn the tricks of vane operation, but the foregoing gives the basic principles of this ingenious gear.

Finally, sails. The sails are the power unit of the yacht and the better and more efficient they are the better the performance of the model. Most racing skippers have their sails made for them by one or other of the professional sailmakers, since it is a job calling for skill and experience, but the following brief outline may guide experimenters.

Most sails today are made from hot-rolled dinghy nylon, but for small models tarantulle may be available. It is essential that the sails are airproof but flexible, hence the hot rolling, and that all materials used match.

Synthetic sails must use synthetic tapes and synthetic thread; mixing different materials means different shrink/stretch characteristics and at best a poor suit of sails. Another essential is that the leach (aft edge) of any sail is cut along the warp of the cloth, i.e. parallel with the selvedge.

Very light sails, spinnakers, etc, are usually made from polythene. Fig. 139 shows how to cut a polythene spinnaker; the seams are cemented and sewn or 'welded' with a soldering iron or similar source of heat.

Paper patterns for the sails are an

excellent idea, since they can be laid on the cloth to effect economy, besides being less expensive if cut wrong at first! The leaches of the sails *must* be parallel with the selvedge of the cloth, and the cloth must be pinned on a board perfectly flat but not stretched in any way, ready for cutting. Fig. 141 shows the shapes to be cut, rather exaggerated; the 'S' bend on the luff should only deviate from the straight by a minute amount — ⅛in. in a 50in. luff. With cotton-based materials, allowance is made for as tiny a hem as can be sewn on leach and foot, using light tension and fairly wide stitches on the machine. Reinforcements are sewn into the corners as sketched (Fig. 142).

The luff is sewn into a linen tape which is creased beforehand. Since the tape will eventually stretch more than the sail cloth it should be slightly shorter than the luff (only experience with the particular materials in use will show by how much), and the sail must be fed into the taut tape so that a series of tiny, evenly-spaced creases appear. These will stretch out as the sail is broken in. A length of tape may also be sewn in a straight line from tack to clew. At the head of the sail, a short length of tape is sewn to reinforce the headboard attachment. The head-board is cut from ivorine or ply, etc, and sewn in place.

Nylon sails are best cut with a hot knife or sharpened soldering iron, guided by a wire or thin wood spline, the heat melting the nylon fibres and leaving a sealed, non-fraying edge. No hems are necessary on leach or foot, and the tape for the luff is best cut as a strip off the same sailcloth, when it will stretch by the same amount as the rest of the sail.

Batten pockets of sail cloth are sewn at right angles to the leach, as the rules allow, and stiff plastic or thin cane battens inserted before sewing up. The sails are completed by providing eyelets, if wire hoops or spiral lacing are to be used (Fig. 143), or hooks for attachment to the jackstay. These hooks are opened-out dressmakers' rustless hooks, eyeleted or sewn in place (Fig. 144). Eyelets must also be positioned at tack and clew of both sails, and at the jib head, for bending. The jibstay is often positioned in the luff hem during sewing.

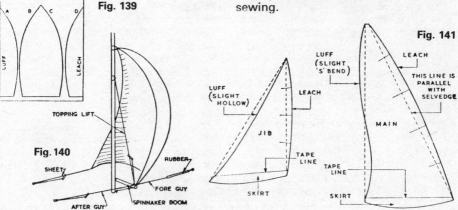

Fig. 139

Fig. 140

Fig. 141

Fig. 142

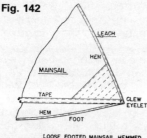

LEACH
HEM
MAINSAIL
TAPE
HEM
FOOT
CLEW EYELET

LOOSE FOOTED MAINSAIL HEMMED
FOOT & LEACH WITH REINFORCED
CORNER & EYELET

Fig. 143

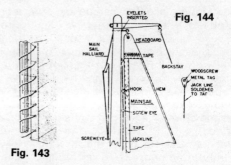

EYELETS INSERTED
HEADBOARD
MAIN SAIL HALLIARD
TAPE
BACKSTAY
WOODSCREW
METAL TAG
JACK LINE SOLDERED TO TAG
HOOK
HEM
MAINSAIL
SCREW EYE
TAPE
SCREWEYE
JACKLINE

Fig. 144

Serious sailing enthusiasts always have at least three suits of sails per yacht, since it is not possible to reef down a model yacht's sails without destroying their efficiency. The second suit normally has a total area of approximately 80 per cent of the top suit, and the third suit a total area of roughly 60 per cent. The sails are identical in every other respect. The top normal suit is often termed the 'working suit' and a 'high aspect ratio suit' is used for light winds. This has the same area but is very tall and narrow, giving greater efficiency but also over-heeling the yacht when the breeze freshens. The average sport sailor will probably only use a working suit, and possibly one smaller suit for windy days, but races are not stopped if the weather deteriorates.

Two A class yachts running with small balloon spinnakers, still in the shelter of a bank at the windward end of the lake but beginning to accelerate.

Chapter Nine

Finishing

Models can be made or marred by the quality of their paintwork, and it is well worth spending a good deal of time on this aspect of building. Care and cleanliness are essential to a good job – plus of course, the patience required in rubbing down and waiting for successive coats to dry.

The inside of any boat must be waterproof since some water is bound to find its way in, and inadequately protected wood will swell when soaked, and shrink when drying out. The least that can be expected from this is interference with the exterior paintwork and, at worst, it can completely ruin the model. Rubbing down inside is not an easy proposition, but if clean brushes and correctly mixed paint or varnish are used, and the interior is thoroughly and completely dusted before each coat, a very passable result can usually be achieved.

It is probably best to use thin polyurethane varnish for interiors, thinned if necessary almost to a water consistency for the first coat or two. It will pool in corners, but will run/soak through small interstices exactly where water would. Pools can be removed by tilting the hull as the varnish begins to set, so that the surplus runs along joint lines and dries into a little fillet. After the first coat it can be brushed out more completely to avoid pooling. Two or three full-strength coats should be used, followed if desired by a coat of light colour which makes cleaning the interior simpler. Even glass hulls are easier to wipe out if the surface is painted. Between coats the brush should be thoroughly washed out in turpentine or white spirit, and washed under a running tap with a detergent.

The outside should now be rubbed down and prepared for painting. If your building didn't quite come up to expectations and a couple of cracks or so are visible, these can be filled with cellulose stopper, epoxy car body filler or a powder filler such as Polyfilla or Tetrion stirred into paint or varnish to make a thick sludge. Rub down when dry with fine glasspaper and wipe off all dust.

For a bright varnished hull use thin varnish as a primer and apply five or six coats of varnish, leaving each to dry hard and rubbing down with carborundum paper as in the following procedure.

In brush painting, apply a priming coat or well-thinned undercoat and when dry give a quick rub over with fine glasspaper. Follow with a slightly thinned undercoat, rub down dry, then apply two coats of undercoat (let the first dry thoroughly), and when the second is dry rub down with 280 grit 'wet-or-dry' paper used with plenty of water and sponging off continually. Rinse off and allow to dry, then examine. Most of the surface will be matt but there will probably be little half-shiny pockets where the paper has not cut down to the paint. The procedure now is to undercoat again, rub down, check, repaint, etc until the entire surface is smooth and unblemished.

For finish coats, use a thoroughly clean brush washed out in hot water and detergent, well rinsed and allowed to dry completely. Stir the paint thoroughly (twice as long as you think necessary!) and pour a sufficient quantity into a clean jar through two thicknesses of nylon tights. Even new paint may have 'nibs' from around the lid. Using a modern gloss paint or enamel should give a reasonable brushing out time, so apply it unthinned but sparingly, brushing at 45° and 135° and finally laying off fore and aft, using the tip of the brush lightly. Modern paints (not one-coat types, which are not very suitable for models) should settle the brush-marks out in 20-30 minutes.

When really hard, rub down with worn 400 paper, wet, and wipe down thoroughly before applying a second, final coat. This may be rubbed down with a fine metal or car polish and finally wax polished.

The same procedure should be followed with epoxy or high-resin polyurethanes (two pot type) except that undercoat is not used; the same paint is applied throughout. Some makes offer a form of filler/undercoat or can be used over cellulose fillers, so check the maker's instructions before buying.

Common faults are impatience, applying old paint which has thickened, applying too much paint, using below-par brushes which were not properly cleaned last time, and leaving the drying hull in a spot where dust can be blown or settle on to it.

Even if a sprayed finish is to be used, the initial coats are best brushed on to get a good solid base. Most of the paint in these early coats is sanded away, but it takes innumerable sprayed coats to fill to a smooth, solid colour since the paint has to be thinned considerably to spraying consistency. Those without spray equipment can make use of one of the inexpensive aerosol-powered spray guns, which can give excellent results, or enamels can be bought in aerosol cans. The commonest fault is to spray too close; the secret is several light coats dusted on rather than trying for full coverage in one coat.

If car touch-up sprays are to be used, check their instructions beforehand, which should indicate appropriate fillers/undercoats for cellulose or acrylic or whatever. Cellulose in particular will react to oil-based undercoats, so care is needed to make the right choice.

Glassfibre (g.r.p.) hulls can be coloured with most finishes, following the procedure on p. 42. Vacuum-formed polystyrene hulls (found in many kits) need similar treatment, but cellulose finishes should be avoided. Rubbing such hulls with abrasive or a cloth to dry them can produce static electricity, making dust stick to them, so they are best wiped over with a painter's tack rag before painting.

Most hulls are painted in two colours,

and the above procedures should be followed except that only one colour at a time is applied, the colour line being masked off to obtain a really neat edge. To determine the correct waterline, mark it off at bow and stern (from the plan or from flotation tests), and block the hull upside-down on the bench so that the points marked are an equal distance above the bench. Mount a pencil, crayon, or stick of chalk sharpened to a chisel edge on a block of appropriate height, and draw the waterline lightly in by sliding the block round the hull (Fig. 145). The mask is a strip of adhesive tape positioned accurately to this line; cellophane tape is perfectly suitable provided that the edge is sealed by running a spoon along to press it firmly down, but with some paints it must be removed with care, by doubling the end back and drawing it off gently (Fig. 146), to avoid lifting the paint. A surer but more tedious job is to use gummed brown paper strip, which must be soaked off.

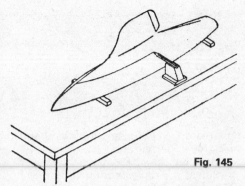

Fig. 145

For best results, the mask should be re-applied for each coat, i.e. with a white and red hull the first coat of white should be brushed on, then the mask removed and the first coat of red applied after masking the white. The whole hull is then rubbed down, and the red re-masked for the second coat of white, and so on. This ensures a smooth paint scheme with no ridge along the colour-line.

Decks are normally finished before fitting since it is easier to line them separately. Occasionally a yacht deck is painted white or ivory before lining, but the procedure is very similar. Ply is frequently too light in colour for a true representation of mahogany or teak planking, so after varnishing the underside several coats the upperside must

be stained. Spirit or water-stain is suitable, and a small quantity should be mixed thin and tried on a scrap of material. Several thin coats will result in a more even colour than one thick one. When the desired hue is achieved, leave to dry thoroughly before applying a coat of varnish primer. Rub down and apply two more coats, rubbing down with 400 paper. Check that a pencil mark can be erased; if not, apply a further coat.

The classic deck lay-out for a yacht is shown in Fig. 147; the king-plank and cover-boards are frequently coloured slightly darker after lining, using scumble or some similar oil-stain, or wood-dye. Planking for a scale type deck will be on the lines shown in Fig. 148. Remember that full-size planking rarely exceeds 6in. in width, and is frequently only 3in. or 4in.; work out a roughly scale width for your particular model. Decks, incidentally, are almost always

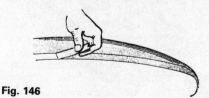

Fig. 146

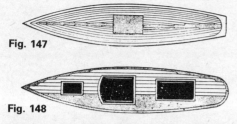

Fig. 147

Fig. 148

cambered, 1:30 for small craft, slightly less for larger vessels.

Mark out the planking with clear pencil lines; a simple tool such as that in Fig. 149 will facilitate this. When the marking out is satisfactory, dust the deck lightly with french chalk to 'kill' any grease and ink the lines over with Indian ink, using a ruling pen. Use a smooth spline about ⅛in. sq. to rule the curves – this is one job where an assistant is useful. Note that the planks are irregularly joggled into the king-plank and/or waterways. Smudges or slips should be allowed to dry, then lightly scraped away with a razor blade. Colour king-plank, etc, if desired.

When dry, dust off, and apply another coat of varnish. Rub down with 400 paper and repeat. Flow the last coat on fairly thickly (i.e. don't brush out *quite* so much) and leave the deck truly horizontal in a completely dust-free room for forty-eight hours.

Wood masts and spars look extremely elegant if french polished before var-

Fig. 149

nishing. Cabin tops, etc, may also receive similar treatment. The grain of the wood should first be filled by rubbing in a plaster of paris paste; wipe off with a damp rag and when set rub down with worn fine glasspaper. The plaster must now be 'killed' with raw linseed oil; wipe off and apply a coat of polish, allow to dry and apply four or five more. Polish up with methylated spirit on a tuft of cotton wool, or varnish.

Painted superstructure requires similar treatment to the hull, using masking where necessary. Small parts and fittings are best painted before assembly.

Some builders find difficulty in choosing a colour scheme for their boats, particularly launch or small cruiser types. The majority of these are painted white above the waterline, and use green, red, or bronze coloured antifouling paint below. Superstructures are most often varnished, decks natural planking, and tops stone or buff colour. Many boats in unsheltered moorings have canvas or linoleum covered tops, painted buff. Ports, handrails, etc, are usually polished brass, other fittings bronze or brass, or painted aluminium, red oxide, or sometimes black, wearing silvery where ropes rub. Well interiors are brown or natural varnish, cabin interiors white or cream with varnished fittings. A look round a harbour or marina will be invaluable, but take a camera and notebook.

Some readers may be surprised that so much trouble over painting is recommended, but the paintwork can make or mar a model's appearance, and when so much time and trouble have gone into the construction, and the model may be expected to give some years of service, an extra hour or two in giving it a proper, durable finish can hardly be considered wasted.

Chapter Ten

Internal Combustion Engines

By far the greatest number of i.c. engines in boats are diesels or glow engines of the two-stroke type, running at fairly high r.p.m., though perhaps not as high as in aircraft use. A typical sport-type 3½cc glow motor will only reach 8-9,000 r.p.m. in the water, and will throttle down to perhaps 4,000 r.p.m., though the difference in boat speed may give the impression of a much wider difference in engine speed.

The two-stroke cycle involves air/fuel mixture being drawn into the crank-

ports, and the incoming fresh gas helps to drive out the exhaust gases. Older engines used sideport (or three-port) breathing, but a rotary crankshaft intake or a rear rotary disc intake is more normal nowadays. A typical (aircraft) diesel with crankshaft intake is shown in Fig. 150 and the different appearances of the three induction systems is shown in Fig. 151. Radio-controlled motors are fitted with a throttle positioned on the air intake tube.

Fig. 150

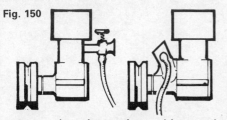

case as the piston rises; this gas is compressed as the piston descends and passes through transfer passages into the cylinder as the transfer ports are uncovered. The piston rises and combustion occurs, while at the same time a fresh charge is drawn into the crankcase. The descending piston first uncovers exhaust ports, then the transfer

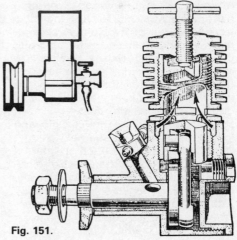

Fig. 151.

71

Fig. 152

Combustion in a 'diesel' arises from the rise in gas temperature as it is compressed by the ascending piston against a contra-piston fitted in the upper part of the cylinder. A screw permits adjustment of the contra-piston position to increase or decrease compression, and there is a needle valve to control the amount of fuel entering the intake from a spray-bar to mix with air being sucked in. Most throttles employ a drilled barrel which controls the amount of air being drawn in, but may also have additional fuel jets for high-speed and low-speed running.

In a glow motor, combustion is initiated by a glowplug, which instead of having a gap as in a car sparking plug has a tiny wire coil joining the electrodes. A 1½v or 2v battery (check — plugs vary) connected to the plug and the engine body causes this coil to glow, when it will ignite the charge of fuel compressed in the cylinder. Once the engine is running the battery is disconnected and the heat from each combustion will keep the coil glowing long enough to ignite the next charge. Differing plugs can be fitted of different heat ranges, having the effect of altering the timing of when combustion begins, but most beginners will be happy with a standard medium plug. The engine also has a needle valve and/or throttle as outlined above for a diesel.

Fuel for diesels is typically equal parts of castor oil, paraffin (kerosene) and ether, which is not particularly fierce in its effect on paintwork etc, except for oil soakage into wood structure. It is nevertheless advisable to apply a thorough coat of fuel-proofer. These engines run comparatively cool and soft-soldered exhausts etc are usually adequate, connected if required by rubber tubing.

Glow motors run on a mixture of castor oil and methanol (methyl alcohol) and frequently employ nitro-methane as a fuel additive. This fuel, and ex-

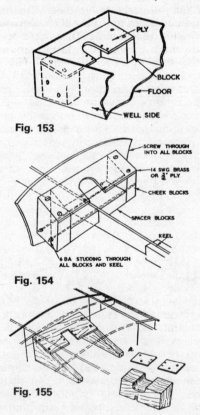

Fig. 153

Fig. 154

Fig. 155

haust products, will attack normal paints and fuel-proofing is essential, except where epoxy or possibly high-polyurethane paints are used. The engines run fairly hot, requiring silver soldering of exhaust systems and silicon tube connectors.

Because the motor delivers its useful power at fairly high r.p.m., with normal direct-drive installations this means a fairly small propeller with small blade area and pitch (q.v.). A flywheel is essential for starting and running, and the motor must be strongly mounted in the hull.

Most modern motors are provided with lugs on each side of the crankcase for fixing (beam mount), but occasionally radial mounting is employed, when the motor is provided with a crankcase backplate for clamping to a ply structural member (Fig. 152). The simplest method of beam mounting is to fit a shelf athwart the boat, with a cut-out for the motor seating. The shelf may be of 3/16in. or thicker ply, or 14 s.w.g. brass sheet, etc, and must be firmly bolted or screwed to blocks glued and screwed into the main structure (Fig. 153); the motor is bolted in its seating, using spring washers and lock-nuts to avoid loosening due to vibration. Alternatively, a short shelf may be used, screwed to cheeks which are bolted, with appropriate spacing blocks, through the keel (Fig. 154). Other methods are sketched in Fig. 155.

In the quest for better silencing, flexible mountings have been developed, the engine mounting plate being bolted to hard rubber or similar blocks with no direct metal connection to the boat's structure. Use of these mounts normally calls for a flexibly mounted propeller shaft (also available commercially) resulting in a reduction of noise and, if

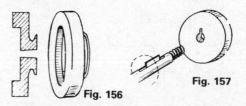

Fig. 156

Fig. 157

anything, a slight increase in performance.

To arrive at the correct position for the motor itself, several factors must be considered. The propeller shaft should be as nearly horizontal as possible, the limiting factors being clearance for the propeller at one end and the flywheel at the other. It is not advisable to use a shaft of more than about 12in. length, since this produces whip and introduces bearing complication. Once the shaft tube is in place, the complete assembly should be made up to assist in determining the exact position of the motor; after fixing the mounting, small packing pieces can be used to bring the motor dead in line with the shaft.

Four factors must be considered in the flywheel — weight, diameter, fitting, and truth. There is no need to exceed about 2¼in. flywheel diameter for any motor under 10cc, and an average weight of about 5oz. can be used for any motor of from 2-5cc. Weight is not critical, as some modellers believe, it merely affects the time taken for the motor to reach maximum r.p.m., and it is better to err on the too-heavy side. The distribution of the weight is important, and it should be concentrated on the periphery of the wheel as in Fig. 156. Modern motors nearly all use a tapered crankshaft for locking, and the flywheel must be carefully fitted to this. Alternatively, a keyway must be cut in the crankshaft and a silver steel key inserted (Fig. 157).

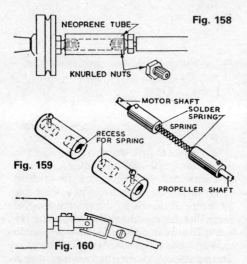

NEOPRENE TUBE

Fig. 158

KNURLED NUTS

MOTOR SHAFT
SOLDER
SPRING
SPRING
RECESS
FOR SPRING

Fig. 159

PROPELLER SHAFT

Fig. 160

The most important factor is truth, for an out-of-balance flywheel will wear the crankshaft bearings oval in minutes, thus losing crankcase compression and reducing the efficiency (and finally ruining) the motor. Flywheels are commercially available to fit just about every known motor, and the builder is urged to buy one from a reputable firm rather than make do with something improvised. These flywheels are all provided with a peripheral groove or an integral pulley for starting purposes, and if you are able accurately to turn your own, something of this nature should be incorporated.

There are several methods of connecting the flywheel to the propeller shaft for driving. A certain amount of flexibility is essential, and there are on the market several flexible or universal couplings which are admirable. One simple idea is to use two knurled fittings provided with hexagonal tips and threaded, one for the engine crankshaft (also holding the flywheel in place) and one for the shaft. A length of thick neoprene tube is pushed over the knurls to make an ideal and virtually permanent coupling (Fig. 158). Another method of doing the same job is to hard solder a few turns of a stout spring between two collars screwing on the shafts (Fig. 159).

More mechanical is the universal shown in Fig. 160, consisting of two threaded collars shaped at their meeting ends and pinned through each other. Fig. 161 shows a dog method; one or two silver steel pins extending from the flywheel face located in notches in a driven disc fitted to the shaft. A simple clutch giving friction drive is detailed in Fig. 162.

The commonest coupling remains the classic ball and socket joint, the propshaft carrying a ball with a cross-pin which fits into a socket on the crankshaft, the socket having notches which engage over the cross-pin. There is no fore and aft location with this form

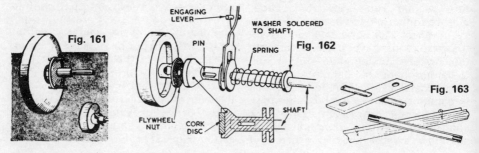

ENGAGING
LEVER

WASHER SOLDERED
TO SHAFT

Fig. 161

PIN

SPRING

Fig. 162

SHAFT

FLYWHEEL
NUT

CORK
DISC

Fig. 163

of coupling, since the two halves are free to slide apart, and the motor and prop-tube must therefore be accurately spaced. Accurate alignment is important with any coupling, so that there are no side loads affecting either shaft.

The propeller shaft should be of stainless steel, at least ⅛in. dia. The usual practice is to install it in a brass tube giving at least 1/32in. clearance all round, with a reamed brass or bronze bush about ⅛in. in length pressed into each end. Warm vaseline can be sucked up into the tube and allowed to solidify before finally pushing the shaft through, and sometimes a greasing hole or Gits fitting is provided on top, at the top end, into which melted vaseline or oil can be poured from time to time. The grease stops water from working its way up.

Occasionally a stuffing box (Fig. 163) is used, with an exposed shaft. This is usually confined to hydroplanes where the hull is not really in the water during operation. Little water finds its way up the tube, in any event, if the shaft fit is good. The advantages are less resistance and ease of fitting a tail-end universal; the propeller thrust must be horizontal on very high speed models, to prevent nosing under.

Propellers for i.c. engines are usually two-bladed, since two blades have proved more efficient (on the whole) at the speeds of rotation involved. Power absorption can be varied by adjusting pitch and/or blade area. Pitch is the theoretical distance moved forward by the propeller (or screw) in one complete revolution (Fig. 164). In fact, propeller slip occurs and the actual distance moved may vary from 60 to 98 per cent of the theoretic pitch.

It will be seen that to design a propeller for maximum efficiency the boat's

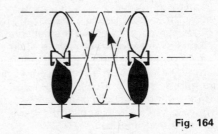

Fig. 164

speed must be estimated, plus the working r.p.m. of the motor. A small calculation will give the theoretical pitch required, from which it is simple to arrive at the likely pitch allowing for slip. The blade angle can be approximated from a geometric drawing such as Fig. 165. Pitch is often expressed in diameters, medium pitch being about 1·2 diameters, coarse pitch from 1·5 upward; thus the diameter can be calculated from the theoretical pitch and blade area must be adjusted until the working r.p.m. estimated are obtained.

There is no difference in the performance of propellers of either hand, and with virtually all motors nowadays rotating anti-clockwise (viewed from astern) a left-hand prop. will be needed. This simplifies attachment, since a normal thread can be used, the water resistance tending to tighten it on the shaft.

Some advantage is gained in 'conventional' boats by using a large three-blade propeller driven at slower speed by gearing the motor down. Unfortun-

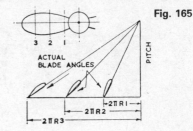

Fig. 165

ACTUAL BLADE ANGLES

PITCH

←2πR1→
←2πR2→
←2πR3→

ately, the mechanical losses in the gears can cancel out the increased efficiency of the screw in the case of small i.c. engines, so there is little point in employing gears unless twin screws are required. In such a case, a gearbox or frame will be necessary, and advantage may very well be taken of the benefits of reduction gearing.

Quite a number of successful boats employ an open gear frame (Fig. 166) with no lubrication system, and some even use brass gears. For long life,

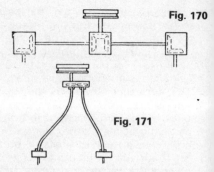

Fig. 170

Fig. 171

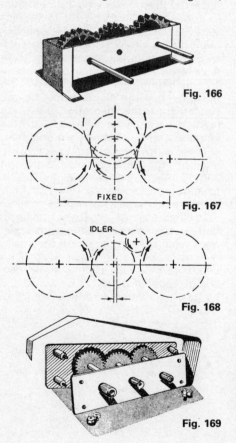

Fig. 166

FIXED

Fig. 167

IDLER

Fig. 168

Fig. 169

however, it pays to invest in steel spur gears, and run their shafts through bronze bushes hard soldered to the frame. A touch of grease now and then will ensure smoother and quieter running. The gear diameters required can quickly be assessed by drawing out the shaft spacing, etc, as in Fig. 167. For contra-rotating shafts an idler gear will be necessary, and this means mounting the motor just far enough off centre to enable the idler to be dropped in (Fig. 168).

Enclosed gear-boxes tend to become a little unwieldy with wide-spaced shafts, but are quite common. Fig. 169 illustrates a simple and reasonably lightweight method of construction. Alternative drives are a double bevel arrangement with three boxes (Fig. 170), though this is rather expensive (7 bevels) and absorbs considerable power, or a flex drive system as sketched in Fig. 171, which is an entirely feasible idea for small motors, but one which is not widely used.

Geared motors are commercially available for high-performance boats, especially in 2½, 3½ and 5cc sizes. The usual layout is to fit a gear to the flywheel, engaging with a gear on a shaft carried beneath the engine. Thus the engine is installed flywheel forward,

A commercial gear-base and engine to fit. Pinion teeth are in groove forward of crankshaft front race. Note aft-facing large exhaust for tuned pipe connection.

which simplifies engaging the starting cord or the belt of an electric starter. In most such engines the lower shaft runs in bearings fitted to the crankcase, but separate mounting plates carrying the shaft, to which a normal engine can be fitted, are available. This geared system should not be confused with the several engines made with a forward flywheel and the drive taken through a short shaft carried by the rear crankcase cover; these are not usually geared.

The question of cooling a motor is a relatively easy one. Actually, sufficient cooling is achieved by heat dissipation through the fins of an aircraft motor if the head is well exposed to the air, but most motors are run inside a boat and watercooling is virtually universal. Fig. 172 suggests a means of fitting a water jacket to an aircooled engine; an alternative is to wind soft copper tube tight to the fins and clamp in place with a hose clip, but most engines are available with water jackets ready fitted.

A small number of boats carry a tank for convection cooling (Fig. 173) but this

Fig. 172

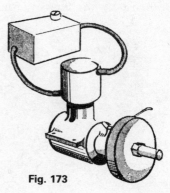

Fig. 173

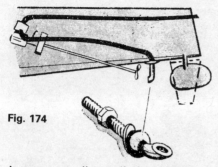

Fig. 174

is more usually applied as a temporary measure when bench running. The usual arrangement (Fig. 174) is to mount a waterscoop behind the up-ward-moving side of the propeller, when water is forced through the jacket even when the boat is held stationary, and is ejected with astonishing power from the outlet. Neoprene tubing is used to connect scoop and outlet to the jacket. The flow of water is normally in excess of what is required, leading to overcooling of the engine, which can reduce efficiency and lead to chemical exhaust residues of a corrosive nature. A small clamp fitted to the outlet pipe should be adjusted to pinch the tube until the water emerging is too hot for comfort on the bare hand. Some modern synthetic oils allow water-cooling to be dispensed with, but use of these is rare.

The exhaust from the engine is messy and oily, and should be led away out-side if possible. It is important to re-member that at no point should the cross-section of the exhaust pipe be less than the total area of the engine's exhaust port(s), otherwise back pressure will be built up, seriously reducing the engine's power.

Most engines nowadays are equip-ped with an exhaust manifold and often a silencer, but two methods of making manifolds or collectors are shown in Fig. 175 and can easily be connected to exhaust pipes with rubber (diesel) or silicon (glow) tubing. An oil trap in the pipe is desirable to avoid water pollu-tion.

All i.c. engines should be silenced and silencers (mufflers) can be bought, though they are not difficult to make. The main object is to lose the high frequencies, achieved by changing the direction of the exhaust flow and allowing expansion of the gases. An assortment of silencers is shown in Fig. 176. Wrapping the silencer in glass-wool (e.g. loft insulation) further cuts down noise.

Initially there was some objection to silencers (one result of which was the loss of use of several waters) on the basis that they absorbed engine power.

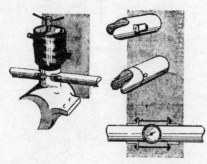
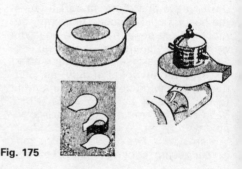

Fig. 175

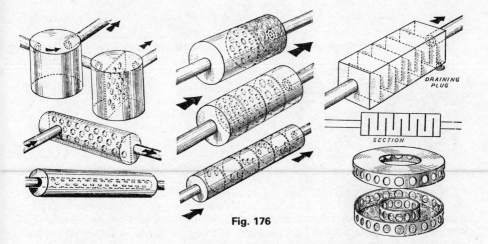

Fig. 176

Certainly the types above may well do so, though the effect is often exaggerated, but the application to boats of the tuned pipe answered criticism since this device reduces noise and increases power output. Briefly it consists of two cones (which may be curved) joined as in Fig. 177. Pressure waves expand on leaving the exhaust, causing the gases to be sucked out and part of the fresh charge to be drawn through. The rear cone then reverses the waves, pushing back part of the charge as the exhaust port is closing. The waves are then reversed again to pass out of the exhaust while the cycle starts again. Tuning is effected by lengthening or shortening the distance between the exhaust port and the first cone, usually by means of a silicon tube connector. The effect is a marked increase in engine speed but this will only occur over a limited r.p.m. starting point, hence the need to be able to tune.

Finally, a thought about tanks. The tank should be mounted as close to the engine as possible, with the fuel level at approximately the same height as the engine needle valve for easy starting. Fuel surge may become important in a high speed, highly manoeuvrable boat, and baffles are sometimes used to obviate this; an alternative (Fig. 178) is to collect the fuel from a small reservoir at the bottom of the tank. This can be made by drilling baffle holes in an empty fuel can and soldering a spare cap, with a pick-up pipe, over the baffle area. Multi-racers often use a split tank straddling the propeller shaft with fuel taken from a Y-connector underneath (Fig. 179).

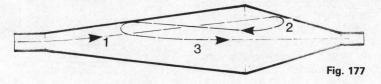

Fig. 177

Tidy installation. Visible are wound square tube cooler, plastic bottle klunk tank and throttle push-rod crossing top of flywheel.

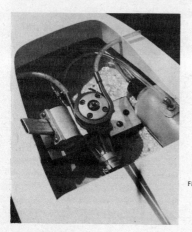

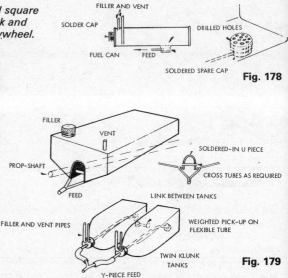

Fig. 178

Fig. 179

Petrol Engines

The major difference with a petrol engine is its form of ignition, which is by a spark created in a coil (Fig. 180) or, increasingly often nowadays, by a magneto built into the flywheel. Additionally the four-stroke cycle is more frequently encountered. Such engines are very much cheaper to run than diesel or glow, and are usually much more flexible, since the timing of the ignition point can easily be varied. Four-strokes are also very much quieter, but the exhaust gases are hotter and silver-soldered exhaust systems are essential. The ignition system must be kept clean and dry to ensure a good, fat spark for easy starting and efficient running.

Nowadays 'spark ignition' is a more correct term than 'petrol', as some of these engines run on methanol. There are growing numbers of four-stroke engines running on glowplugs and methanol, a spin-off from the engines

developed since about 1980 for R/C aircraft use. Though these respond well to throttle, they should not be confused with actual spark ignition motors.

The upper limit of 30cc for spark ignition was raised some years ago by the M.P.B.A. to 35cc, to allow the use of an inexpensive 34cc two-stroke industrial motor of modest performance. This higher figure was adopted internationally, leading to hand-built high-performance engines delivering 6-7 h.p., considerably more than many small 'full-size' engines!

Fig. 180

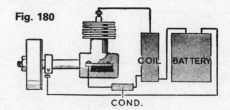

Chapter Eleven

Steam Engines

One of the cheapest power plants to run is the steam engine, and, of course, there is the added attraction of there being something scale about it. It has the disadvantages of being rather hot and messy to operate, and is rather heavy and bulky for the power produced; nevertheless, it is very fascinating and there are few other forms of power which can be started up to provide three or four hours non-stop cruising for the outlay of a few pence. There are two usual types of steam engine, the oscillator and the slide valve, but there are many variations in boilers and lamps, so it is perhaps advisiable to examine them one by one.

Oscillating Engines

The name of these motors originates from the fact that the cylinder(s) oscillate(s) when the engine is running. Instead of the normal gudgeon pin fitting, the connecting rod is rigidly fixed to the piston, and as the crankshaft rotates the cylinder is rocked from side to side. The back side of the cylinder is ground to a flat face which bears on a valve block, also flat-faced. The valve block is provided with inlet and exhaust ports with which the cylinder inlet and exhaust ports register (Fig. 181).

Because of the relatively simple construction, oscillating engines are usually inexpensive to buy, and will work off quite a low steam pressure, such as can be obtained from the simplest type of boiler. The simplicity is carried over to the lubrication system, which usually consists of a vertical oil container through which the steam passes on its way to the cylinder. Some of the steam condenses, sinks, and dispaces oil which then flows into the cylinder.

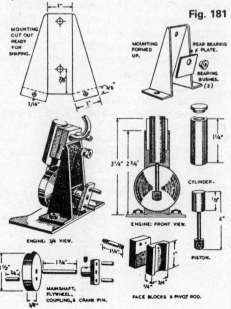

Fig. 181

Fig. 182

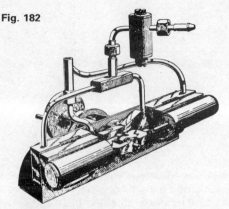

Power output is not large, but will vary with the accuracy with which the engine is made, and the steam pressure. A ⅜in. bore and stroke motor on 12-15lb. pressure will on average provide sufficient power for a 24-30in. model weighing approximately 4lb.

Multi-cylinder oscillators can be built, most popular being the horizontally-opposed twin layout (Fig. 182). A 30-36in. hull weighing about 8lb. can be satisfactorily powered on 15lb. steam with a ½in. bore and stroke twin-cylinder engine.

Slide Valve Engines

The second type of steam engine widely used in all sizes of model from 30in. up is the more efficient slide valve design. The piston arrangement is con-

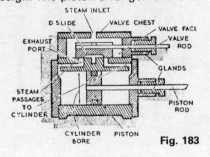

Fig. 183

ventional and the cylinder fixed, but an eccentric is fitted to the crankshaft and operates a valve-rod connected to a slide moving in a valve-chest. The slide is milled out to allow passage of steam between two pairs of pipes as shown in Fig. 183. Steam admitted to alternate sides of the piston provides double action. Steam losses are very slight compared with an oscillator, and slide-valve engines are generally considered to be more of an 'engineering job', suited to serious work.

The power available from these engines is considerable, an example being a single cylinder, ¾in. bore and stroke, working on 45-50lb. pressure, which is quite adequate for a 4ft. boat weighing about 45lb. Multi-cylinder arrangements are quite common, the cylinders normally being in line. If the pistons are *not* synchronised in timing, the engine will be self-starting; single cylinder engines can stop at the bottom of the stroke.

Boilers

The simplest form of boiler is that shown in Fig. 184, consisting of a water container in a casing which allows sufficient room beneath for a burner, which may be a methylated spirit lamp or a small tray on which is burned a solid alcohol fuel such as is sold for some types of camping stove.

Developments of this are usually concentrated on improving the heat supply or lowering the overall height. The 'chicken-feed' burner in Fig. 185 achieves both these ends, since it permits greater flame spread for the same duration with a shallower tank than Fig. 184, the means being an external supply tank for the spirit. Since the burner is of necessity as low in the boat as possible, the tank is higher than flame

Fig. 184

Fig. 185

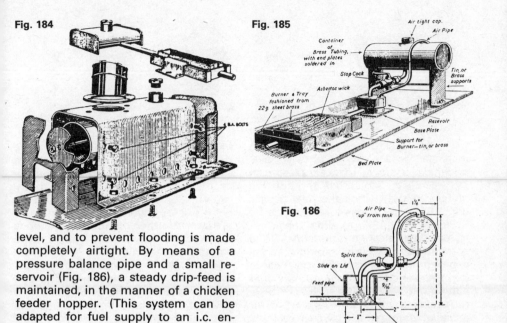

Air tight cap.
Air Pipe
Container of Brass Tubing, with end plates soldered in
Stop Cock
Tin or Brass supports
Asbestos wick
Burner & Tray fashioned from 22 g sheet brass
Reservoir
Base Plate
Support for Burner—tin or brass
Bed Plate

B.A. BOLTS

Fig. 186

Air Pipe "up" from tank
1¼"
Spirit flow
Slide on Lid
Feed pipe
3"
9/16
2"
1"
Spirit kept at this level by air pipe

level, and to prevent flooding is made completely airtight. By means of a pressure balance pipe and a small reservoir (Fig. 186), a steady drip-feed is maintained, in the manner of a chicken feeder hopper. (This system can be adapted for fuel supply to an i.c. engine.)

Fine model of the ex-Thames tug Cervia *in present colours. Two-cylinder steam engine just visible; superstructure detaches in two main units. Radio sealed away in stern.*

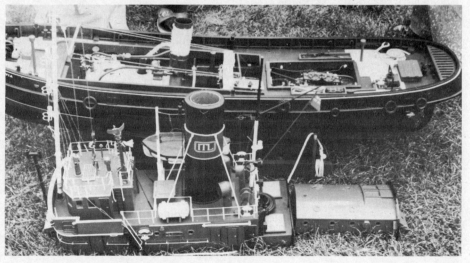

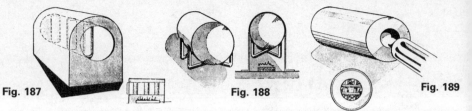

Fig. 187   Fig. 188   Fig. 189

The next step in boiler efficiency is to increase the area of heating surface, and this is achieved in its simplest form by placing vertical tubes through the boiler, through which the heat passes (Fig. 187). Next, cross-tubes can be introduced (Fig. 188), to allow the water to circulate through the flames. The culmination of these methods is the centre-flue boiler, in which a blowlamp flame is played through a tubular boiler equipped with cross-tubes (Fig. 189).

Specialists in steam work go in for real engineering practices, such as pump fed boilers and high efficiency units operating on the flash steam principle. In this system a coil of stainless steel tube is heated almost red hot by one or more blowlamp flames, and water is fed in at a controlled rate. Needless to say its vaporisation is instantaneous, and the volume of steam produced is quite extraordinary. Models powered with engines running off such boilers do in fact compare quite reasonably in speed with racing models powered by the more frequently encountered petrol engines. The subject, fascinating as it is, is just a little beyond the scope of this present book.

Petrol or paraffin blowlamps, used for many years in more powerful steam generators, have given way to a large extent to butane gas cylinders, using burners adapted from portable gas stoves or paint strippers. These are more consistent and reliable than the earlier blowlamps but where maximum steam generation is important petrol/paraffin is still preferred by many experts. Coal firing is occasionally seen, but more for novelty than efficiency.

Any of the coupling methods described in the previous chapter are suitable for steam engines, but installation is a little different. By far the best system is to mount the entire boiler and engine assembly on a single aluminium or alloy plate, which can then be fitted into the hull by four single bolts. The surrounding woodwork should be painted with a heat-proof paint, or, in the region of extreme heat, it may be insulated with asbestos paper, attached using waterglass as an adhesive. If radio is to be fitted, it must be an entirely separate unit, sealed from heat, steam, water, oil, etc. If the engine is fitted with valve gear, reversing and speed control are possible by radio, always remembering the desirability of two or more out-of-phase cylinders.

One feature of steam is that power output does not vary with r.p.m. to anything like the extent of i.c. engines, and the r.p.m. available are considerably lower in any event. This means that a fairly large three-blade prop. can be used – as a very rough rule of thumb, 1in. of diameter for every ¼in. of engine bore. Gearing down is not normally necessary.

Chapter Twelve

Electric Motors

Probably no range of motors offers the scope in power output available from electric motors. Miniature units weighing little more than 1oz. can be used in boats as small as 8in. in length, and at the other extreme are motors suitable for powering six and seven foot models. The most frequent use of electric power is in boats of less than 36in. l.o.a., although many larger models use it for its cleanliness and ease of operation and control. In small sizes dry batteries may be used, though they are nowadays rather costly.

Large motors can be extremely expensive unless rechargeable accumulators are used, in which case the initial expense is fairly heavy, but the subsequent running costs negligible.

Lead acid batteries are sometimes used, particularly in large scale-type models where ballast must be carried in any event. Scooter batteries are popular as being smaller and much more compact than car batteries, yet with useful capacity. It is possible to obtain sealed lead acids, or ones in which the acid is gelled to make it unspillable; care must be taken with the normal free acid type, and they must be kept clean and corrosion-free and regularly charged to avoid deterioriation.

By far the commonest power source is, however, the nickel cadmium cell or nicad. These are normally sealed units giving 1·2v per cell (as opposed to 1·5v for lead acid or dry batteries) and they will stand a considerable amount of neglect or abuse. A characteristic is that they will deliver current at an almost steady rate until almost discharged, when the current dips abruptly, while lead or dry cells tend to fall off gradually from peak output.

The capacity of any cell is given in ampere/hours, e.g. 1·2v, 1·2 a/h, which means that nominally the cell will deliver 1·2 volts at 1·2 amps for one hour; five cells will deliver 6v at 1·2 amps for one hour. In fact the cells would be exhausted some time before the end of the hour, but if the load was ·3 amps and not a continual drain (i.e. switched off occasionally) then 4 hours (4×·3= 1·2) could well be achievable. At the other extreme, if the load was, say, 3·6 amps (three times capacity) although notionally this should be available for 20 minutes, in practice about 10 minutes is more probable.

Thus the amp/hour capacity quoted is a guide and the slower the current is extracted the more chance there is of the nominal capacity being realised. The other use of the a/h figure is to indicate charge rate: usually 1/10 of the capacity is the maximum recommended for charging, which in our example is ·12a (120 milliamps). The charge rate is required for about 1/3 more time than might be expected, because of internal changes in the cell, so that a charge of 120ma is applied not for 10 hours, but for 13·3, and this is usually rounded up to 14 hours.

Motor power is usually expressed in watts (amps×volts=watts) but this is watts input and the power delivered is affected by the motor efficiency, i.e. watts output=watts input×motor efficiency, drive losses, etc. Increasing the load on the motor, by fitting a larger propeller or one of greater pitch, increases the current drawn, thus shortening running time per charge. There is such a variation in motor performance that it is virtually impossible to lay down general guidelines; the best advice is to look through published designs (your local library should be able to obtain recent volumes of *Model Boats*) to see what motors are fitted in models similar to your project. If you are a member of a club, or are fortunate enough to have a nearby model shop with boat experience, direct advice should be available.

The same recommendation must be made for propellers, which always require some experimentation, though for sport or scale models it can be said that if the motor gets hot, the load is too great and a smaller or finer pitch prop should be tried. Direct-drive props will be small − smaller than scale − and frequently two-bladed rather than three. If a scale three or four blader is to be fitted, gears are virtually automatically required.

Modern motors are almost without exception of the permanent magnet type, reversible by simply changing current polarity. A simple motor control can be made by mounting a microswitch either side of a servo output disc, shaping the disc into a cam. This, with the appropriate wiring, will give centre off and full ahead and full astern (or tap only part of the battery for half astern) when the servo is operated. Speed controllers operated by a servo, or sometimes simply plugged into the servo socket on the receiver, can be bought to give infinite speed adjustment from stop to full speed ahead or astern; circuits for home construction have also appeared in model magazines.

Speed or multi-racing models usually use only an on/off switch operated by radio and can be quite impressive, both in appearance, with banks of nicads providing the current, and in performance, which can match the speed of all but the top glow-engined boats. Whereas 45-50 watts (12v×4a or 6v×8a) may propel a sport cabin cruiser of, say, 30in. length and 5lb. weight at 3 m.p.h. or so (a normal walking speed) or a 5ft. battleship at scale speed, a fast model will be running at 24v, 16a or more (say 400 watts) and the motor will be watercooled. The cells will be exhausted in three or four minutes (these also get hot) but there is a vented type of nicad which can be fast-charged, perhaps at 5 amps or more for 10 to 12 minutes, using either a mains charger or a car battery as a charging source. This is a specialised area in which ignorance can be dangerous, but published information is available.

The advantages of electric power − clean, quiet and simple operation − are slightly offset by the limited running time per charge, but with two charged packs of cells, or the use of fast-charge cells, the handicap is not severe and where weight is not critical, so that a battery of large capacity can be used, an electric boat can be run for several hours between charges.

For maximum efficiency the average

electric motor should drive a propeller through a reduction gear (except for speed models) since usually the most efficient running speed of any electric motor, in terms of power output and current drain, is at least three times the speed at which it could be expected to drive a useful propeller. Fortunately, for most installations, inexpensive brass gears are perfectly adequate, and, in fact, an old clock will frequently supply all that is necessary. Geared motors, or gearboxes, can also be bought. Alternatively, belt-driven pulleys can be used with entirely satisfactory results, particularly where two shafts are taken from the same motor. Pulleys are available in many sizes, or can be turned up, or laminated from washers of differing diameters bolted or soldered to the shafts. Contrarotation is easily arranged by crossing the appropriate belt, and no coupling troubles are likely to arise. If couplings are required, any of those in Chapter Ten are suitable, or the simplified arrangements shown in Fig. 190 may be used. Miniature motors will drive efficiently through a length of insulation stripped off lighting flex and forced on the shafts. With electric power, accurate shaft alignment is vital for good performance and long battery life.

The usual method of installation is to screw or bolt the motor to a block or blocks glued and screwed to the main structure. Washers may be used to pack the motor to the correct height; the couplings should run as truly as possible since power is wasted otherwise. Cylindrical motors without mounting plates can be held in a shaped bed by means of a metal strap or (even in high performance models) stout rubber bands. Even when gears are used it pays to connect the motor to the drive gear with a flexible coupling, which

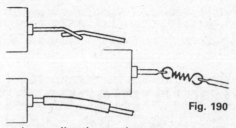

Fig. 190

reduces vibration and wear.

Wiring should be neat and firm, with soldered joints where possible. Care should be taken to keep the installation free of water and excess oil. It is customary to have a permanent switch built into the fixed superstructure, either placed as unobtrusively as possible, or disguised as a deck fitting such as a capstan, although a radio-operated switch, especially as part of a speed controller, can be substituted.

Batteries should be easily removable for cleaning and inspection, but may be charged in place in the hull if a suitable harness and socket are provided. For prolonged storage (i.e. a month or more) it is best to remove them and store separately.

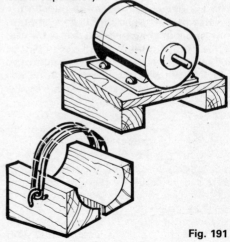

Fig. 191

ChapterThirteen

Hydroplanes and Special Models

One of the simplest forms of boat is the airscrew-driven hydroplane, which uses an aircraft motor and propeller and thus avoids much of the complication of a water-cooled conventional submerged propeller installation. There are some drawbacks, in that some local authorities and some clubs prohibit the use of such models in free-running or radio form, because of the possibility of injury from the almost invisible propeller, but with care (and a silencer) they can provide safe fun. Operation where there are swimmers or children paddling is obviously out of the question.

They are usually light and simple models, borrowing much from model aircraft techniques, and employing balsa and ply structures. They can be run free on isolated ponds, or tethered if very high speeds are desired. Design

is aimed at producing a light planing hull usually employing a step, having sufficient beam to resist rolling induced by torque. Directional stability is achieved by side area both above and below water, and longitudinal stability (pitch) is induced by providing a hull with a C.G. (centre of gravity) fairly well aft, the engine having slight down-thrust to hold the bow down, and the shape of the planing surface being arranged to provide up-thrust. Correct relation of these factors produces a damping effect which irons out pitching or porpoising.

Tethered airscrew hydroplanes (Class B1) are the fastest of all models and have a strange dragonfly beauty; they certainly do not resemble any normal boat. Anyone attracted by these is urged to visit a regatta where they are competing (check with the M.P.B.A. secretary, with a S.A.E.) since there is much to be learned from exponents of the art and they will be most helpful to genuine enquirers.

Racing Hydroplanes
As with any model designed for 'ultimate performance', a racing model hydroplane demands considerable skill and patience to achieve good results.

Fig. 192

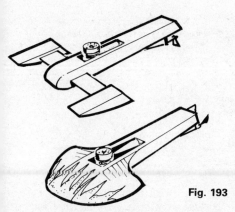

Fig. 193

The modern craft of this type normally employs three point suspension, i.e., the model is in contact with the water at three small points only when at speed. These points are usually provided by the trailing tips of two sponsons at the bow (Fig. 193), and the extreme stern of the boat – a total area of a mere square inch or so.

A line is always used to tether the model to a fixed point, and so fast are some hydroplanes that the engines are designed to run at settings taking into account the spray drawn into the engine – spray still in the air from the previous circuit! All-ply, all-metal, or mixed ply and metal construction may be used, and the static buoyancy is usually marginal, just enough to keep the boat on the surface.

An important factor in design is the shaft and screw arrangement. The screw thrust *must* be horizontal or the boat will dive or back-flip, and this means a second universal at the lower end of the shaft. Normally open shafts and stuffing boxes are used, as mentioned earlier, and the propeller is fitted in a bearing which is carried on a fitting variously known as an A-frame, skeg, or prop-bracket. This, of course, has to be

a very rigid fitting, and is usually filed from a casting or from the solid, with in the latter case the tube bearing and attachment lugs brazed on (Fig. 194). Props are usually only half immersed when running.

Engine installation follows standard practice, except that there is rather less room than usual. Tanks for circular running are, of course, a different proposition, since centrifugal force will throw the fuel to the outside, and the effort required to suck fuel will vary with the quantity remaining in the tank. This is the reason for a hydroplane engine 'peaking' or 'coming in' at one point during the run. The feed pipe must obviously run to the outside rear corner of the tank, and high, narrow tanks reduce the sideways head of fuel when in motion. Experimentation is usually necessary to determine the best type of tank and its actual position.

Two-point attachment of the bridle is customary; the fore-and-aft position of the line connection can be determined by suspending the model on its side and balancing it exactly horizontally. It is safest to have the imaginary extension of the tether passing through the model's C.G. in the vertical plane. The bridle attachment points must be firmly anchored to the internal structure, and the bridle is best made from piano wire or stranded cable, the ends being made off as in Fig. 195.

Fig. 194

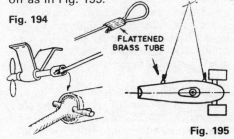

FLATTENED BRASS TUBE

Fig. 195

Example of scale R/C hydroplane at an American show. These models are usually surprisingly heavy, but fast all the same.

Radio Hydroplanes

These have been popular in North America for several years and have recently attracted a small following in other countries. They can be very fast (70-80 m.p.h.) but are not good at turning, so competitions tend to be either for straight speed 110 yard dashes or round a very large (440 yard) oval course. Three-point suspension is normal, the aft point often being the downward-moving blade of the surface propeller. While separate sponsons are occasionally seen at the fore end, frequently the bow of the boat is one wide fairing with sponsons mounted beneath. Scale models of the big full-size inboard hydroplanes, now rarely seen outside the U.S.A., are quite feasible and there are kits for several.

With the introduction of high-performance outboard glow engines there was some activity with outboard hydroplanes but, although such boats are still made, they have not made any significant gain in popularity.

Rubber-driven Models

Rubber strip, though nowadays fairly expensive, is a somewhat neglected power source for boats, but is quiet and clean and can easily give runs of 4-5 minutes duration. Rubber-driven models have the advantage of adjustable power – it is a simple matter to add or remove a loop or two of rubber. For high speed dashes two or more motors are used, driving the propeller through a gearbox (brass gears are adequate) as in Fig. 196. Even single-motor models are better for the incorporation of a gearbox, but chiefly in respect of duration of run (Fig. 197).

Many types of otherwise orthodox models can be rubber-driven by the system shown in Fig. 198. A tunnel is

Fig. 196

Fig. 197

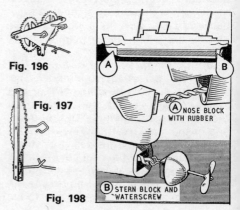

A

B

(A) NOSE BLOCK WITH RUBBER

(B) STERN BLOCK AND WATERSCREW

Fig. 198

provided through the hull, with removable plugs at each end. The stern plug carries the propeller and bearing, the bow plug the forward rubber anchorage and a winding loop. Flood-holes are provided so that the tunnel quickly fills when the boat is placed in the water. Large, fairly coarse pitch propellers are used for duration, small props with coarse pitch for speed. Refer to model aircraft literature for guidance on making up and using rubber motors.

Clockwork Models

These have effectively disappeared except for some very small toy boats, but some amusement can be had by modifying an old clock mechanism such as a discarded alarm clock. Apart from the mainspring and its associated gear train all the redundant parts can be removed and one of the wheel spindles extended by soldering on a brass tube, drilling the clock plate to pass the tube (Fig. 199). A propeller cut from tinplate will enable quick adjustment of pitch, or rapid substitution of a larger or smaller prop, to balance boat speed against running time.

Scale Sailing Models

The main problem with scale models of sailing vessels was outlined in Chapter One, but there are other factors. There is little resistance to sideways motion of a shallow hull in the top two or three inches of water, while there is considerable wind resistance in the masts and rigging, etc. Thus a scale model will make leeway (i.e. be blown downwind) to a much greater extent relative to forward travel than a racing yacht, which will have a deep fin and less drag in its rig. A reasonable yacht will sail at about 40° to the wind, but few scale sailers will do better than 60°.

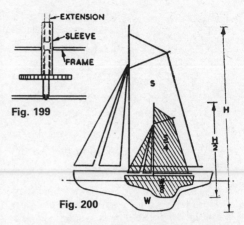

Fig. 199

Fig. 200

To achieve stability in most instances, some form of false keel and external ballast is needed; the volume of the keel can be made sufficient to offset the weight of the ballast if the hull is already of scale weight, so that the vessel floats on its proper waterline, though usually the model is underweight and would need some ballast anyway. The false keel may extend along the hull (Fig. 201) or be centralised (Fig. 202) and will improve the sailing qualities by reducing leeway. A keel of 27 cu. in. will allow an extra 1lb.

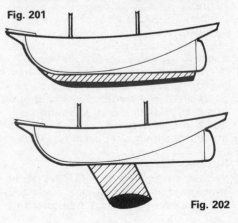

Fig. 201

Fig. 202

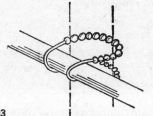

Fig. 203

of ballast without changing the waterline.

A fore and aft rig will always prove a better sailer in model form than any design with square sails, especially to windward. If the square sails can be furled and the model sailed on, for example, headsails, staysails and spanker some progress towards the wind should be achieved, but otherwise a square-rigger is only likely to sail across or downwind.

The physical difficulties of trimming an all square-rig model are usually overcome by securing the yards with rather free-fitting parrels (which can be simply lengths of copper wire threaded with tiny glass beads (Fig. 203), their vertical positions being ensured by the lifts. The yard braces are faked so that

all yards are inter-connected, and one master on each side will trim every one. Incidentally, the most frequent fault in scale sailing models is over-sparring and over-rigging. An air of delicacy is essential, and it is far better to make spars and rigging too light than too heavy.

Submarines

Model submarines are particularly attractive, and lend themselves especially to rubber drive. If electric power is used, the access hatches must be screwed in place over a rubber seating, and a switch should be provided externally, over which is cemented a cut-off baby's teat, so that the switch may be operated through the rubber while still remaining waterproof.

The surfaces which make a submarine dive are hydroplanes (Fig. 204), and these can be operated by a worm gear (running off the propeller shaft) from inside, to produce a succession of diving and surfacing, or the planes can be spring-loaded to 'dive' position and fitted with an arm (Fig. 205) on which is mounted a drag-plate (a scrap of celluloid) which can be adjusted in height or size to provide a submerged cruise or resurfacing. Whatever system is used, if the model is made just positively buoyant, it will always surface at the end of the power run. A safety measure is a soldered-up tin, disguised as a gun mounting, equipped with a coiled line, and stuck in place with soap (Fig. 206). If the model is caught in weeds, or remains submerged for any other reason, the soap will slowly dissolve and allow the tin to surface.

With fore and aft hydroplanes both set to dive gently, boat's way will slowly slide it under. Motor time-switch allows resurfacing.

Fig. 204

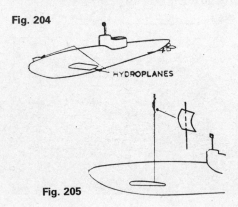

HYDROPLANES

Fig. 205

By the way, to answer a common question, it is possible to radio-control a completely submerged model, but only if the model's aerial is completely insulated from contact weith the water. Sophisticated R/C models are made with ballast tanks which can be flooded, then pumped or blown by compressed air or freon gas, or even effervescent tablets released into the tanks. Another system is to flood a tank and seal it before release, so that the sub submerges immediately; a small pump driven from the propshaft gradually empties the tank and the boat slowly surfaces. Air for this can be drawn from a snorkel or a half-inflated balloon in

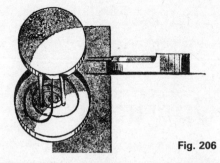

Fig. 206

the tank will expand as the water is pumped out, or another section of the hull can be pressurised with a bicycle pump and air leaked from this.

Attractive barque photographed at a scale sailing regatta. For expert modellers – and will only sail downwind.

Advanced scale model of a Type IX U-Boat Casing and much of hull is free-flooding, ballast tanks are pumped with model fuel pumps.

Chapter Fourteen

Operation

It is a pity for romantics that a boat's first contact with the water usually comes some time before the last coat of paint is dry and the last detail fitted; however, it is far more practical to test trim during construction, before alteration of the position of a component becomes a major operation. The time for this is after the initial two or three coats of paint and, if possible, before permanent attachment of the deck. Mark the waterline at stem and stern with pencil ticks, and place components, or equivalent weights, in correct positions, and check that the hull floats true. Very few models are larger than can be accommodated in the household bath, but if you have difficulty, many clubs have measuring tanks, or of course, the model can be checked in a pond.

If, after completion, ballast is required to bring the boat down to her marks, or to correct trim, determine the required amount and its position by stacking cut chunks of lead in place, then melt the lead into a convenient block and screw it in place in the hull as low as possible.

Prepare everything for the initial outing with care — tools, fuel or fresh batteries, rag, sponge, starting cord if necessary, spares, etc, and a pole and a sorbo ball with forty or fifty feet of twine attached. Establish a routine, since nothing is more frustrating than arriving at the water to find some essential item omitted. On arrival, check wind direction, current (if any), weed patches, and retrieving possibilities. A light, wide

Squatting or kneeling and gripping hull with knees makes single-handed starting easier. Crossing cord is unnecessary once experience is gained.

rake is often useful to clear small areas of surface weed.

Steam, electric, clockwork, or rubber power need no comment on starting procedure. I.c. engines need a starting cord, which may be a 3ft. length of blind cord or ³/₁₆in. leather belting or, best of all, a leather bootlace or similar thong. This is not wound round the flywheel groove (as with a full-size outboard), but merely passed beneath the flywheel, located in the groove, and crossed once (Fig. 207). The transom of the boat is gripped between the knees, and an assistant grips the bow (some people start single-handed by jamming the bow against a tree or kneeling on the model on its stand). The cord is gripped in both hands and the fly-wheel 'rocked' backwards and forwards until the engine is firing. Light tension is then kept on the right-hand end and the left-hand pulled sharply away. If the motor doesn't start, the process is repeated.

Control over a diesel is obtained by adjustment of the contra-piston and needle-valve, and the running settings after starting, on land, may be considerably different from the settings required when the boat is placed in the water, where the r.p.m. are much lower. The slower speed means later ignition, hence the contra-piston must be raised, and decreased carburetter draught means less fuel, hence the needle must be opened. These adjustments must be made as the boat is lowered in, or just beforehand — it depends on the individual engine and lay-out.

Spark ignition motors are controlled by an ignition advance and retard lever and a needle-valve, and although not so critical as diesels, some adjustment of these controls is usually necessary. Glow engines have only a needle control, but are quite touchy on this, and

Fig. 207

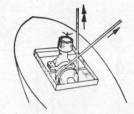

will need increased fuel as the revs. are slowed.

Rudder settings for cruising will vary with local conditions, but if a straight run is required it must be remembered that propeller torque will tend to crab the boat's stern, giving, normally, slight right turn. Once on its way, the model should be watched for incorrect trim — lifting or slamming of the bow, etc. Ballast should be added, or component positions altered to cure this.

A telescopic or sectionalised pole is often of great assistance where reeds or shallows exist, and for long range retrieving a sorbo ball, pierced and

Fig. 208

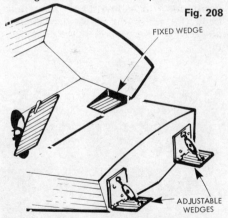

Torque reaction rolls the boat starboard side down and causes right turn. Wedge glued on and cut away to trim levels boat. Transom flaps or tabs do the same but are adjustable for differing water conditions.

95

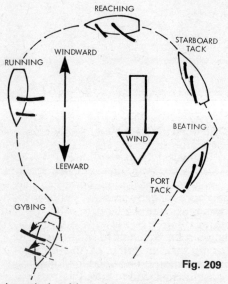

Fig. 209

threaded with twine, which may be thrown over the model and drawn towards shore with every hope of entangling the model and recovering it, is most useful. The sponge in the kit is used for extracting unwanted water which may have found its way into the hull.

Any type of model should be thoroughly sponged down with clean fresh water after a day's sailing; the engine, etc, should be thoroughly cleaned and dried, tanks emptied, and, in fact, the whole boat left in a clean and 'safe' condition.

Sailing Craft

It is important that a sailing model floats exactly on her designed waterline, otherwise she will never give her best performance. A table of weights, or at least a total displacement, is given with any reputable design, and this should be adhered to as closely as possible, any variation being adjusted by means of the amount of lead. A few ounces under the total required weight is a little advantage, since this means that trimming ballast may be incorporated.

After assembly at the pond-side, note the wind direction and walk to the downwind bank. Trim the main boom to swing about 7 or 8° off centre and the jib 9-10°. Lock the rudder central. Point the yacht 40° off the wind and ease gently away. It will continue on the

A class yachts ready to start a run, with following pairs moving to a ready position. Perfect trim is essential.

Marbleheads racing with vane. Four pairs can be seen and it looks as though all are guying from a lee bank.

course started, or turn up into wind and come into irons (boat stopped, sails shaking) or turn away from the wind and dither until it can be retrieved. In the first case you are very lucky, in the second the mast is too far aft and should be moved forward, in the third the mast needs moving back. Make the adjustments and repeat until on either tack there is the slightest tendency to come to the wind, the yacht probably slowing but turning away and picking up speed again. In this trim 1° of rudder held by vane or radio should see the yacht 'pointing' as high as possible while travelling at a fast speed ('footing').

The same mast position will hold for all courses, but individual yachts will vary on what sail settings will produce the best results on different headings. If possible sail against a 'trial horse' so that you can see which adjustments work best, the 'horse' being another yacht of similar size and proved performance.

For sailing to windward (called 'beating') the sails are usually sheeted well in, about 5-7° to the centre line of the hull, but *not* pulled in so hard that there is no movement. The jib ideally should be a degree or so freer than the main and if the boat will not sail well thus the mast should be moved or its rake altered, though never rake the mast forward. For reaching (across wind) the sails need to be eased out to around 40°, but this will vary from boat to boat, and for running (down-wind) free the sails right off to 90° or as close to it as the rigging allows.

Sailing a yacht is an art, and one in which a minute of demonstration is worth ten written pages. The budding skipper can do no better than take his yacht along to one of the yacht clubs listed in the appendices, or at least pay a visit to see other models being sailed. Even if there is no local club, have a day out and travel to the nearest, and don't be shy to introduce yourself and seek advice. Yachting enthusiasts are always delighted to meet a 'convert', and will usually gladly give their time and experience in order to see him on the right path.

Chapter Fifteen

Radio Control

The subject of radio control for model boats requires a whole book to itself, and it is therefore hoped that electronic wizards will be forbearing if only the basic outlines are described here. As on previous occasions in this book, it is necessary to consider power boats and sailing craft separately in the particular, although many of the comments made apply to either class in general. First, however, for the benefit of those who have yet to taste the joys of radio control, let us take brief and non-technical look at the actual radio side.

Radio

Modern radio control equipment consists of a transmitter operated by the modeller, radiating signals which are picked up by the receiver in the model, decoded and applied to the appropriate servo, which is the electro-mechanical device which translates the radio signal into movement of the respective control. Apart from inserting batteries (or charging up the nicads if the equipment is rechargeable) no technical knowledge is required – it is simply a matter of switch on and it works. The average boat needs only two functions (which means two servos), one for rud-

der control and one for engine or sails. Usually the transmitter has two sticks, the right-hand one spring centred and moving horizontally, controlling the rudder, and the left-hand one ratcheted, moving vertically, for engine throttle, electric motor speed/reverse, or sails in/out. Each stick has adjacent to it a trim control which biases the centre position. As an easy example, if a boat does not run straight when the rudder stick is central, the trim control can be used to correct it and the spring centring will then always return the stick to the corrected centre.

Apart from the sticks and trims, a basic transmitter will have a telescopic aerial, an on/off switch, a meter showing battery state, possibly a charging socket, and facilities for crystal changing. This last requires explanation, and it is basically the means by which several sets can operate simultaneously without mutual interference in the narrow frequency band allocated for use by model radio.

A quartz crystal can be ground to operate on a very precise frequency and can be introduced into a radio circuit so that the frequency of transmission is equally precise. A matching crystal in

Simple radio in a small trawler. Left-hand servo is fitted with a printed circuit switch board controlling motor.

the receiver will respond only to that frequency, so that if sockets are provided in the transmitter and receiver, matched pairs of crystals can be plugged in, i.e. it is possible by changing both crystals to alter the frequency on which one's equipment operates. One word of caution – the receiver crystal signal is mixed with another signal (for various technical reasons) and the crystal is thus not identical with the transmitter crystal. The little two-pin canisters containing the crystals are clearly marked 'Tx' and 'Rx', so make sure they are plugged in correctly.

Different countries may be allocated different frequencies, and in Britain the '27 meg. band' is for surface models and the 35 for aircraft only. There is also a UHF wave-band, but most boats operate in the 27 band, the equipment being considerably cheaper. The band actually extends from 26.975 to 27.275 megaHertz and is divided into approximately 50 kH spaces and colour-coded. More selective modern radio has allowed further division into 25 kH spacing, these frequencies being known as 'splits' and coded by the col-

ours either side. The full list is:

Colour	Tx Freq.	Rx Freq.
Black	26.975	26.520
Brown	26.995	26.540
Brown/Red	27.025	26.570
Red	27.045	26.590
Red/Orange	27.075	26.620
Orange	27.095	26.640
Orange/Yellow	27.125	26.670
Yellow	27.145	26.690
Yellow/Green	27.175	26.720
Green	27.195	26.740
Green/Blue	27.225	26.770
Blue	27.255	26.800
Purple or Blue/Grey	27.275	26.820

It is probably sufficient for the average model boater to have four sets of crystals, three solid colours and one split. This means that he will normally be able to run his boat even if several others are operating. Most clubs use a pegboard, from which appropriately painted wooden clothes pegs representing the frequencies are issued; if you haven't the peg you don't switch on your radio, and you return the peg immediately you have switched off after a run so that someone else can use the frequency.

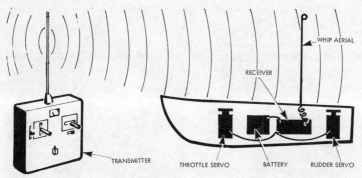

Diagram of normal two-function radio for a power boat. Throttle servo may physically operate a throttle (i.c. engine) or an electric speed controller, or it may be a self-contained electronic speed controller.

Maintenance of the radio is a question of cleanliness and care in plugging and unplugging, plus keeping the batteries charged. An occasional check for dirty or damaged connectors and, particularly, the receiver on/off switch is all that most users bother with; an occasional check by the manufacturer's service agent is desirable and is usually money well spent. Faults can most conveniently be isolated by swapping servos or checking against another modeller's identical equipment, but anything not obvious is best handled by the service agent.

With the cost of dry batteries, nicads represent a sound investment, despite the initial cost of the cells and a charger. Many of the low-priced 'dry' sets include a charging socket so that nicads can be fitted at a later date, when finances have recovered from the initial purchase, but it is usually cheaper to buy the set as rechargeable at the outset.

Installation

The on-board equipment for the average power boat consists of receiver, battery and two servos, and their instalation depends to some extent on the type of model and, perhaps, whether the servos are waterproof or at least water-resistant. For a racing boat all the radio is best enclosed in a waterproof box or compartment, push-rods from the servos passing through watertight glands and the on/off switch operated by an additional push-rod through the lid of the box or the hatch cover. Changing crystals usually means unscrewing the container, unless the socket is sited under a removable watertight bung, in which case it may be convenient to mount the switch and charging socket under the same secondary cover.

Equipment for a yacht: fourth on-board item is in this case a sail winch. Note frequency coloured ribbon on transmitter aerial.

Other models might have just the receiver and battery in a watertight box (plastic food boxes are often used), wrapped in sponge rubber and with aerial, charging and servo leads cemented through holes in the box. Silicon bath sealant is excellent for this sort of job. The servos can then be mounted adjacent to their controls, or in any convenient position. Once again, the box will have to be opened to change the crystal, but it is likely to be a clip-on lid rather than one screwed down on to a greased soft rubber gasket.

Electric competition models may well follow either of these systems, but more sedate scale types, less likely to ship quantities of water, are often seen with the radio components unprotected, other than being mounted off the floor of the hull, so that any water which may get in will swill harmlessly beneath.

Steam models tend to throw some oil and condensate about and the radio is best screened off, either in a box or in a separate compartment sealed from the engine bay. With simple steam plant such boats are usually single-function rudder only, due to the difficulty of applying any meaningful control over the engine. Reducing the steam flow by a form of throttle will reduce engine r.p.m., but the risk is that the piston will stop at bottom dead centre, requiring a manual movement to restart it. Twin cylinders with unsynchronised pistons should be free of this possibility, but the engine is then not quite so simple.

A method of obtaining speed and steering control, including going astern, without varying engine speed or direction is sketched and is suitable for i/c and steam engines. This is known as a Kitchen rudder, and consists basically

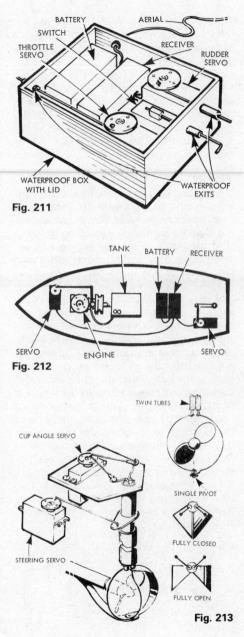

Fig. 211

Fig. 212

Fig. 213

101

of two cups fitting round the propeller. The cups can be swung from side to side to provide steering, or progressively closed to produce backwash which will slow or stop the boat, or, when the cups pass a critical point, actually cause it to move astern. Note that the whole unit is swung by the steering servo, the speed control servo being mounted on a plate soldered (or epoxied) to the main tube.

Yachts

It is possible to sail a yacht with rudder control only but not very efficiently. It is also possible to have automatic sheeting worked by a vane switching gear, so that the yacht is simply set on the desired course by rudder application and the sails automatically set themselves.

Most people prefer to have full control of sheets and helm, and the commonest method is to have sychronous sheeting, i.e. both jib and main operate together and always maintain the same relative angle to each other. The sheets (usually attached to points on each boom an equal distance from the boom's pivot) are controlled by a winch of some sort and a conventional servo operates the rudder. Winches may be of the drum or lever type, and in the case of a drum the normal system, evolved from racing experience, is to use the drum to drive an endless sheeting line extending along or below the deck. The line is secured to the drum, wrapped five or six times round it, then runs to a

Fig. 215

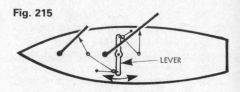

LEVER

pulley which may be at the bow or only a foot or so ahead of the drum; the line then returns to the opposite side of the drum and is again wound half a dozen turns and made off on the drum. Operation of the winch thus drives the line (forward on one side and aft on the other) over a travel of, usually, 9-12in. and back again as the winch is reversed. The sheets from the booms pass through sheet leads on the hull centre line and are then secured at convenient points to the sheeting line, making sure, of course, that both sails move in the same direction – not as obvious as it may sound! (Fig. 214).

With a lever winch the lever normally rotates horizontally, above or below deck, and the sheets pass through centre leads, then through leads fore and aft of the lever ends and are then hooked or tied to the lever (Fig. 215). The extra leads effectively double the sheet travel.

Other systems of sheet control may involve a winch operated by a second servo and having its own battery supply (used most often on larger yachts) or a second servo used to switch a home-built geared winch (old alarm clocks have been used) or to switch a motor driving a threaded rod on which a jockey travels fore and aft. By far the majority of yachts, however, use a commercial drum or lever winch plugging into the receiver in place of a second conventional servo and running off the same batteries as the receiver. It is possible to achieve a weight of under

Fig. 214

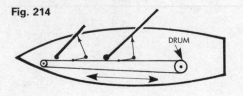

DRUM

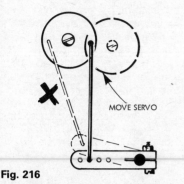

MOVE SERVO

Fig. 216

10oz. (250gm) for a complete radio installation powerful enough to sail a Marlbehead or 10-rater under any wind conditions.

Yacht installations vary, some stowing all the equipment in a watertight box or compartment, some ensuring that the hull (especially a glass-fibre one) is watertight, the only holes being sheet exit points, which can be raised above deck level. Since weight distribution is important, only a small hatch is normally cut in a lightweight deck, to preserve structural integrity. Distances between equipment and controls are often much more than in power boats, and a small secondary hatch may be sited over the tilller; sometimes the servo lead is extended and the servo mounted adjacent to the rudder beneath this hatch. It is common to see the rudder push-rod and tiller mounted above deck (the rudder tube then passes right through the hull, minimising the chances of internal leakage) and, frequently, the winch drum and sheeting system is above deck.

Control Links

Most servos use a disc or short arm for output, rotating through 90° or so, i.e. 45° each side of neutral. Some may have a little more travel, and some can have linear output, where the output arm slides back and forth in a straight line, which can simplify link-up, though few such servos seem to be used in model boats.

Linkages are usually by wire push-rod, with clips screwed on the ends of the rod to engage in holes in the output disc or arm and the tiller or whatever. The sprung clips ensure that the rod does not become disconnected and, by screwing them in or out, allow length adjustment. Ideally the rudder push-rod should make a right-angle with the tiller, which should in turn be exactly aligned across or along the hull, so that equal rudder movement occurs either side. If the servo is the wrong sense for correct rudder application (relative to the Tx stick) and the Tx does not include servo reverse switches, the servo should be moved bodily rather than angling the push-rod to the opposite side of the output disc, which would give unequal rudder movement.

Wire push-rods can be bent up, with turned-over ends to engage the holes and a thin spring wire keeper soldered on (Fig. 217) and a Z or V bend which can be opened out or closed slightly with pliers to adjust the length.

Though wire push-rods are used quite often on engine throttles, if the servo is at the back of the boat and the throttle lever on the engine well for-

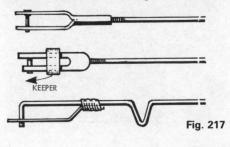

KEEPER

Fig. 217

Fig. 218

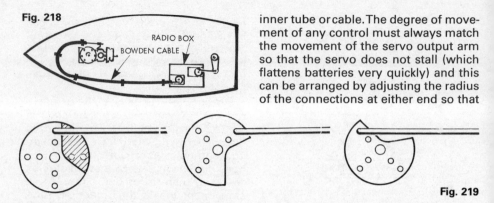

RADIO BOX

BOWDEN CABLE

inner tube or cable. The degree of movement of any control must always match the movement of the servo output arm so that the servo does not stall (which flattens batteries very quickly) and this can be arranged by adjusting the radius of the connections at either end so that

Fig. 219

ward, a better linkage may be obtained with a 'snake'. Snakes are stiffish tubes with a smaller stiff tube, plastic rod, or stranded wire sliding inside; a Bowden cable is similar. The outer tube must be secured to the hull structure at intervals, to prevent it moving or distorting, and can be curved round to reach awkward spots, though the straighter and/or smoother its run the less power will be needed for the servo to move the

the control reaches its extreme position at the extreme of servo travel. It is often necessary to cut away part of a servo output disc so that the connecting clip does not foul it (Fig. 219).

One further linkage is the 'closed loop' type where both sides of an output disc or symmetrical output arm are connected to both sides of the tiller (or other suitable control) by cords or, preferably, thin wires. The advantage is that the control is always pulled, whereas a single push-rod pulls in one direc-

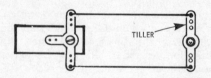

TILLER

Fig. 220

tion and pushes in the other, which can cause it to bow and thus prevent full control application. (Fig. 220)

Visible in this photo is a small bracket which locates and locks the end of the throttle snake casing. Tapered flywheel allows motor to be mounted slightly lower.

Aerials

Always use the Tx aerial fully extended and held as nearly vertical as possible. The Rx aerial is usually provided as a coiled wire which must be uncoiled and stretched straight; its length is important as it constitutes part of the tuning circuitry. Shortening the aerial will cause a departure from perfect tuning and reduce the operating range, so if any alteration is made, by, say, using a piano wire whip aerial, ensure that the total length remains unaltered. A whip aerial on a boat gives the best reception and can be folded or sprung and clipped down for transport or engine starting,etc, but be careful to make a really good, clean connection between the external aerial and the aerial wire of the receiver. It is advisable to keep the aerial away from electric motors or electrical wiring carrying heavy current.

As a generalisation, modern radio will control a model up to and beyond the range of visibility, where you can't see what's happening anyway, and an average at least two hours' operation should be obtained from one charge or one set of dry cells.

There is, of course, much more to radio than the above notes have covered, but they do embrace the more important points and should help you to enjoy your boating, which is the main object of this book.

Radio Marbleheads running down to the lee mark in light wind. Full-size skippers find radio racing fascinating.

Quick reactions and good mechanics are necessary in multi-racing, which is fast and furious, especially at pit stops.

Appendix One

Model Yachting Classes

Model yachting in England and Wales is controlled by the Model Yachting Association, one of the leading countries of the International Model Yacht Racing Union (see Appendix Three). The classes sailed include those used internationally and these classes are identified below. Normally the prefix letter 'R' is used to denote radio control where a class is used for both radio and free sailing. In order of size:

1. 36in. Restricted (36R, also R36R)

A British class, basically requiring the hull (with fin and ballast) to fit inside a box 36×11×9in. Displacement is limited to 12lb., sail area unrestricted. A similar class in the U.S.A., the 36/600, limits length to 36in. and sail area to 600 sq. in. but there are no other restrictions.

2. Marblehead (M, 50/800, also RM) International

The most popular class world-wide for both vane and radio racing. Length limited to 50in. (with ¼in. tolerance), sail area to 800 sq. in, and jibhoist to 80

The 36R is the smallest official class and these radio skippers give a good idea of size. Racing is close in this class.

Myriads of sails at a World Championship for both RM and R10R classes attracting over 100 entrants from a dozen countries.

Below, a sequel to the RM photo on page 105. The two leading boats are beating for the weather-mark while the other six still struggle.

per cent of main, which in turn may not extend more than 85in. above deck. Modern Ms tend to have 9-11in. beam and 15-18in. draught with displacement between 10 and 16lb.

3. **6-Metre** (6m, R6m) International Very popular in the 1920s and '30s, this class does not now attract wide support. The rule is complex, basically the I.Y.R.U. 6-metre rule scaled to give ½ scale models. Average size is about 54-56in. l.o.a., displacement in the region of 20-25lb.

4. **EC12m** International This is a one-design radio class based on a 60in. l.o.a. tank test model of a projected 12m design. G.r.p. hulls must be obtained from approved suppliers and there are fairly tight restrictions on sails etc. Popular in the U.S.A., where it originated, and there are a few boats elsewhere, mainly in England, Australia and Sweden.

5. **10-rater** (10r, R10R) International The oldest rule, originating over 100

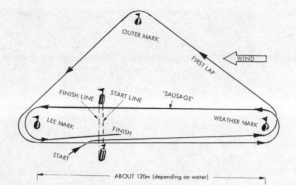

OUTER MARK
FIRST LAP
WIND
FINISH LINE START LINE 'SAUSAGE'
LEE MARK WEATHER MARK
FINISH
START
ABOUT 120m (depending on water)

years ago but adjusted from time to time. Produces the fastest yachts and is the second most popular class for radio. Basis is the simple formula SA×LWL÷7500=10, where SA is sail area (sq. in.) including mast profile and LWL is load waterline in inches. Long and slim yachts result, e.g. 52in. w.l., 1440 sq. in.,

or 60 in. w.l., 1250 sq. in., plus overhangs of perhaps 18in. total, beam and draught (both unrestricted) perhaps 11-13in. and 16-20in., displacement 18-25lb.

6. **A Class** (A, RA) International

The largest class. Fairly complex rule which produces similar performance from a wide range of yachts from 25 to 80lb. displacement (1960s average about 50-60lb., 1980s average 35-40lb.). Maximum and minimum displacement, quarter beam length and freeboard are controlled by subsidiary formulae; main one is

$$\frac{L+\sqrt{S}}{4} + \frac{L\times\sqrt{S}}{12\times\sqrt[3]{D}} = 39\cdot37$$

where L is load waterline length (plus half any excess in quarter beam length), S is sail area in sq. in. and D displacement in cubic in. Because of size (length is usually 7ft. or so, or over 2m) these yachts are not as easy to transport as smaller, lighter classes and apart from one week of vane racing annually in England international events are few.

One of the authors' yachts on first trials, the RM Harem. Although functional, some concession to scale appearance has been made.

RA yachts moving out for the start count-down. The third yacht is moving fast in the opposite direction and the windsurfer is obligingly staying clear.

Full rating rules, sailing rules, etc are available from the Hon. Publications Secretary, M.Y.A., at time of printing C. Jackson, 5 Crofton Court, Cypress Road, South Norwood, London SE25 4BB. Please send S.A.E. with enquiries, or first contact nearest club.

For the sake of completeness mention should be made of a further international class, the 10/40, which has never been sailed in English-speaking countries and now attracts only limited support in France. Length is limited to 1m and sail area to 40dm^2. Several countries have 'domestic' classes not sailed elsewhere, some sail only radio classes, mostly RM and R10R. Two unofficial classes acknowledged by the M.Y.A. are the *Mickey Finn*, a 36in. radio una rig, and the 575, a 17½in. radio model of limited performance but used by M.P.B.A. members for fun races.

Appendix Two

Power Boat Classes

The major international body for power boats is Naviga, originally a European organisation but now accepting affiliation from other countries. In Britain control is by the Model Boat Association (see Appendix Four), which is a member of Naviga. Some countries (notably in Eastern Europe) have one national authority covering all types of models, for which reason Naviga includes some yacht classes, using I.M.Y.R.U. rating rules. American power-boat classes and courses are different from the rest of the world and have little following outside the U.S.A., although a few individuals build U.S.-style models and, in an attempt to make meaningful comparisons, the M.P.B.A. has an annual 'records day', when American courses are laid out. Naviga classes are:

A1 – Tethered hydroplanes (screw or propeller), i.c. up to 2·50cc.

A2 – Tethered hydroplanes (screw or propeller), i.c. up to 5·00cc.

A3 – Tethered hydroplanes (screw or propeller), i.c. up to 10·00cc.

A straight-runner scores a bull at a Naviga Championship at Duisburg. The rowing boat tows them in when the compulsory timeswitch cuts the motor.

A scale frigate easing its way round a tight course. Points are lost for touching or missing out any of the hazards.

B1 – Tethered airscrew hydroplanes, i.c. up to 2·50cc.

(Course for all classes 500m, 5 laps on a 31,846mm tether line.)

C-1 – Static models from rowing boats to sailing ships.

C-2 – Static model ships and boats with mechanical propulsion.

C-3 – Models of ship installations, ship parts, harbour and ship models and dioramas.

C-5 – Miniature models in classes C-1 to C-3 with an overall size of 1250mm or smaller.

E – Straight runners, course as illustration (page 12), divided into:

EH – Merchant or pleasure ships;

EX – Warships;

EX – Freelance.

(EH and EK 100 pts. for construction, 100 for steering, 20 for scale speed. EX judged on steering only.)

German model of the Ruhr. Warships are usually good for straight running but difficult to steer precisely in radio events, especially in wind. Plenty of work for detail lovers!

F – Radio classes, courses standard as sketches, sub-divided into:

F1-V3·5 – Speed, water or airscrew, engines up to 3·50cc.

F1-V6·5 – Speed, waterscrew, 3·50-6·50cc.

F1-V15 – Speed, waterscrew, 6·50-15·00cc.

F1-E1Kg – Electric speed, total weight up to 1kg.

F1-E2 – Electric speed, over 1kg.

F2-A – Scale ships, length 600-1100m.

F2-B – Scale ships, length 1101-1700mm.

F2-C – Scale ships, length 1701-2500mm.

F3-V – l.c. steering, any engine (waterscrew), up to 3·5cc (airscrew).

F3-E – Electric steering.

FSR-E2kg – Multi-racing, waterscrew, up to 2kg.

FRS-E2kg+ – Multiracing, waterscrew, over 2kg.

(Up to 12 boats, 15 minute races for 2kg, 10 minutes for over 2kg.)

FSR-V3·5 – Multi-racing, waterscrew, up to 3·50cc.

FSR-V6·5 – Multi-racing, waterscrew, up to 6·50cc.

FSR-V15 – Multi-racing, waterscrew, up to 15·00cc.

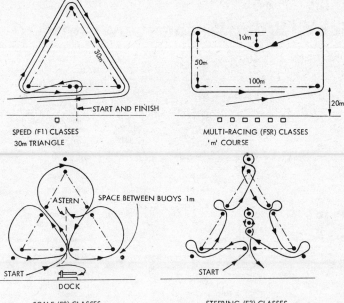

SPEED (F1) CLASSES
30m TRIANGLE

START AND FINISH

MULTI-RACING (FSR) CLASSES
'm' COURSE

SPACE BETWEEN BUOYS 1m

ASTERN

START

DOCK

SCALE (F2) CLASSES
CLOVERLEAF COURSE

START

STEERING (F3) CLASSES
CHRISTMAS TREE COURSE

FSR-V35 – Multi-racing, petrol fuelled, 15-35cc.
(M course, 3-12 boats, 30 minute races.)

F-6 – Team demonstration event, novelty, etc, 12 minutes.

F-7 – Individual demonstration, one operator only.

British Classes

In addition to the above classifications, the M.P.B.A. recognises four hydroplane classes, though two of these coincide with the Naviga classes. They are:

Class A – I.c. engines within a limit of 30cc, steam-driven boats restricted to an all-on weight of 16lb.

Class B – I.c. engines within a limit of 15cc, steam-driven boats restricted to an all-on weight of 8lb.

Class C – I.c. engines within a limit of 10cc, steam-driven boats restricted to an all-on weight of 5lb.

Class D – I.c. engines within a limit of 5cc.

Straight-running boats are not restricted in any particular way (they correspond to EX class) except that they must not exceed 12 m.p.h. or use an engine larger than 35cc. General rules require engine silencing, drive by water-reaction, etc.

Radio boats have had a number of changes while this side of the hobby has been establishing itself; it is safe to make models to Naviga classes, however, since these fit into any rules which may foreseeably be adopted by the M.P.B.A. In fact the trend is towards standardisation on Naviga lines.

Appendix Three
Model Yachting Association Clubs

Districts are shown as follows: Northern (N); Midlands (M); S/Western (W); Eastern (E);
Metropolitan & Southern (S).

Andover & District MBC
B. D. J. Brown
29 Woodlands, Overton,
Basingstoke, Hants. RG25 3HN. (S)
Tel: 0256-770145.

Appledore MPC
M. Evans
2 Orleigh Close, Buckland Brewer,
Bideford, N. Devon EX39 5EH. (W)
Tel: 023-72-3421

Ashton RYC
A. Worsley
15A Back Moor, Mottram,
Hyde, Cheshire EX39 5EH. (N)
Tel: 061-646-2376

Birkenhead MY & PBC
K. Jones
8 Marline Avenue, Bromborough,
Merseyside L63 0RJ. (N)
Tel: 051-334-1969

Birmingham MY & PBC
P. E. Lock
Flat 14, York Road, Erdington,
Birmingham B23 6TE. (M)
Tel: 021-382-1708

Bournville MYC
P. J. Somers
171 Bournville Lane,
Birmingham B30 1LY. (M)
Tel: 021-451-2404

Broads R/C MYC
Mrs A. Batch
60 Fairfax Road, Norwich,
Norfolk NR4 7EZ. (E)
Tel: 0603-55417

Chelmsford RYC
G. Bantock
35 The Paddocks, Witham,
Essex CM8 2DR. (E)
Tel: 0376-516248

Cheltenham R/C MYC
B. Decker
24 Longway Avenue, Charlton Kings,
Cheltenham, Glos. GL53 9JL. (W)
Tel: 0242-33751

Chiltern MYC
D. J. Robinson
206 Little Marlow Road, Marlow,
Bucks. SL7 1HX. (S)
Tel: 06284-2505

Chippenham MYC
I. P. Walters
131 Queens Crescent, Chippenham,
Wilts. SN14 0NW (W)
Tel: 0249-651893

Clapham MYC
M. J. Peppiatt
13 Stanley Road, Carshalton,
Surrey SM5 4LE. (S)
Tel: 01-647-6701

Cleethorpes MYC
G. Griffin
19 Rowston Street, Cleethorpes,
S. Humberside DN35 8QS. (N)
Tel: 0472-692191

Cleveland MYC
D. M. Hackwood
10 Grangewood, Coulby Newham,
Middlesborough, Cleveland TS8 0RT. (N)
Tel: 0642-595577

Danson MYC
G. W. Clark
30 Carston Close, Lee,
London SE12 8DZ. (S)
Tel: 01-318-3737

Decoy MYC
A. Hinkins
'Town Farm', Abbotskerswell,
Newton Abbot, S. Devon TQ12 5NX. (W)
Tel: 0626-2279

Doncaster MYC
K. Brown
79 Ellers Avenue, Bessacarr,
Doncaster, S. Yorks. DN4 7DZ.

Eastbourne MYC
N. Sylvester
18 Highwoods Avenue, Little Common,
Bexhill-on-Sea, Sussex TN39 4NN. (S)
Tel: 042-43-2750

East Yorkshire MYC
F. Lovell
226 Queensgate, Bridlington,
E. Yorkshire YO16 5RW. (N)
Tel: 0262-73670

Etherow MBC
J. T. Morrison
277 Buxton Road, Macclesfield,
Cheshire SK11 7ET. (N)
Tel: 0625-616643

Fleetwood MY & PBC
P. Whiteside
7 Princess Way, Fleetwood,
Lancashire FY7 8PG. (N)
Tel: 039-17-78219

Gosport MY & PBC
Mrs J. Bullivant
8 Melville Road, Gosport,
Hants. PO12 4QX. (S)
Tel: 070-17-88410

Guildford MYC
R. J. Pease
5 Springfield Road, Camberley,
Surrey GU15 1AB. (S)
Tel: 0276-26234

Harrow Lodge MBC
F. Benzing
37 Albert Road, Romford,
Essex RM1 2PS (S)
Tel: 0708-60927

Harwich & Dovercourt MYC
G. Bantock
35 The Paddocks, Witham,
Essex CM8 2DR. (E)
Tel: 0376-516248

Hereford & Worcester MYC
J. A. Valentine
40 Hampton Park Road, Hereford,
Herefordshire HR1 1TH. (W)
Tel: 0432-275263

Hove & Brighton MYC
L. Baker
4 The Herons, Shoreham,
Sussex BN4 5UJ.(S)
Tel: 07917-61939

Kings Lynn Soc. Mod. Eng.
L. J. Garrett
48 Fenland Road, Wisbech,
Cambs. PE13 3QD.(E)
Tel: 0945-754102

Leeds & Bradford MYC
G. Barrett
10 Grange Avenue, Shipley, Bradford,
W. Yorkshire BD18 4BT. (N)
Tel: 0274-585233

Leicester RYC
A. G. Drury
93 Forest Road, Huncote, Leicester,
Leicestershire LE9 6BH. (M)
Tel: 0533-863786

Lincoln & District MYC
I. Stevenson
3 Field Close, Nettleham, Lincoln,
Lincs. LN2 2RX. (M)
Tel: 0522-751611

Mansfield & District BC
N. K. Simmons
'Lynden', Howard Street, Sutton-in-Ashfield,
Notts. NG17 4DD. (M)
Tel: 0623-512705

Medway Marine Mod. Soc.
D. G. Jones
4A Knockhall Road, Greenhithe,
Kent RA9 9HJ. (S)
Tel: 0322-846483

Milton Keynes Mod. Soc.
B. Somerville
4 Parkway, Wavendon, Miltor Keynes,
Bucks. MK17 8UH. (M)
Tel: 0908-583372

Model Yacht Sailing Association
J. Parkins
91 Dove Park, Hatch End, Pinner,
Middlesex HA5 4EE

Newcastle-on-Tyne MYC
N. Pattison
35 Cranwell Drive, Wideopen,
Newcastle-on-Tyne NE13 6AS. (N)
Tel: 0632-366265

New Forest R/C MYC
T. Fuller
5 Chetwynd Drive, Bassett, Southampton,
Hants. SO2 3HY. (S)
Tel: 0703-766055

Norfolk & Norwich MYC
P. Goodson
49 Antony Drive, Norwich,
Norfolk NR3 4EW. (E)
Tel: 0603-410126

North Wales MYC
G. Kirkham
152 Old Highway, Colwyn Bay,
Clwyd LL28 5YE.(N)
Tel: 0492-2840

Petersfield & District MYC
C. G. Gallup
'Inwood', Hill Brow, Liss,
Hants. GU33 7QG. (S)
Tel: 073-082-3238

Plymouth MSC
F. Attwood
30 Lanhydrock Road, St. Judes,
Plymouth, S. Devon PL4 9DL. (W)
Tel: 0752-665691

Poole MYC
H. M. Studd
64 Broadwater Avenue, Parkstone,
Poole, Dorset BH14 8QH. (S)
Tel: 0202-744397

Rugeley MYC
L. D. Edwards
3 St. Aidans Road, West Chadsmoor,
Cannock, Staffs. WS11 2PG. (M)
Tel: 05435-79217

Ryde MYC
J. A. Buttigeig
2 Gordon Road, Newport,
Isle of Wight PO30 2EU. (S)
Tel: 0983-528052

Shrewsbury MYC
M. Element
9 Longbridge Close, Shrewsbury,
Shropshire SY2 5YD. (M)
Tel: 0743-67087

Solent R/C MYC
D. S. Watson
9 Edward Road, Hythe, Southampton,
Hants. SO6 6BD. (S)
Tel: 0703-843488

Southgate MYC
I. Taylor
115 Mayfield Avenue,
London NW12 9HY. (S)

South East Essex MYC
J. Cleveland
41 Highfield Avenue, Benfleet,
Essex SS7 1RY. (E)
Tel: 0702-558616

South London MYC
W. Jupp
83 Sussex Place, Slough,
Bucks. SL1 1NN. (S)

Southampton MYC
W. Downie
18 Eastbourne Avenue, Shirley,
Southampton, Hants. SO1 5HT. (S)
Tel: 0703-785935

South Wales MYC
J. R. Gibbs
4 Smeaton Close, Rhoose, Barry,
S. Glam. CF6 9FU. (W)
Tel: 0446-711123

Swansea & District MYC
G. O. Griffiths
4 Wimmerfield Close, Killay, Swansea,
W. Glam. SA2 7DE. (W)
Tel: 0792-5541

Three Rivers MYC
G. Wright
10 Winchester Road, Northwood,
Middlesex HA6 1JF. (S)
Tel: 09274 26530

Warrington MYC
I. Grainger
9 Brickhurst Way, Woolston, Warrington,
Lancs. WA1 4LG. (N)
Tel: 0925-39443

Wicksteed MYC
T. A. College
117 Winfield Street, Rugby,
Warwickshire CV21 3SH. (M)
Tel: 0788-67947

Woodbridge MBC
Miss S. Banyard
11 Through Duncans, Woodbridge,
Suffolk IP12 4EA. (E)

Woodley (Reading) MYC
Mrs M. E. Curtis
21 Wallace Close, Woodley, Reading,
Berks. RG5 3WH. (S)
Tel: 0734-663512

Woodspring MYC
N. Rothwell
20 New Cheltenham Road, Kingswood,
Bristol, Avon BS15 1TJ. (W)
Tel: 0272-615497

YM 6m OA
A. A. Jupp
83 Sussex Place, Slough,
Bucks. SL1 1NN. (S)

Hon. Gen. Sec.,
R. Gardner
6 Rowner Close, Rowner,
Gosport, Hants. PO13 0LY.

INTERNATIONAL MODEL YACHT RACING UNION
Secretaries of member National Bodies

(A) Argentina
Federacion Argentina de Yachting
Modelismo
Guillermo Jose Medin,
1208 Hipolito Yrigoyen,
3519 DPTO 4,
Capital Federal,
Argentine.

(KA) Australia
Australian Model Yachting
Association (AMYA) Incorporated.
Norman D. Lorimer,
129 New World Avenue,
Trevallyn,
Tasmania 72,
Australia.

(B) Belgium
Royal Model Yacht Club, Antwerp.
Frans Fierens,
MD IR Haesaertslaan,
76, B-2610, Wilrijk,
Belgium.

(BL) Brazil
Secretary Uniao Brasiliera De Veleiros
R/C
Jose Edwuardo Vianna,
Rua Sao Carlos 1170,
Bairro Floresta 9000,
Porto Alegre-RS-Brazil.

(KC) Canada
Canadian Model Yachting Association
R. J. Button,
342 Lorindale Road,
Oshawa, Ontario,
L1H 6X4,
Canada.

(D) Denmark
Dansk Modelbads Union
N. Harvey Hansen,
Egelokkevej 51,
Tooring,
7400 Herning.

(K) England
Model Yachting Association
Roy Gardner,
6 Rowner Close,
Rowner,
Gosport,
Hants.
PO13 0LY.
England.

(F) France
Federation Francaise De Voile
Michel Lahure,
2 Avenue General De Gaulle,
94240,
L'Hay Les Roses,
Paris,
France.

(G) Germany
Deutscher Segler Verband
Joachim Kullick,
Ansgarinsweg 3,
2000 Wedel Holstein,
West Germany.

(H) Holland
Nederlandse Model Zeil Organisatie
(Nemozo)
Paul Prior,
Straat Van Magelhaens 36,
1183 HD Amstelveen,
Holland.

(KH) Hong Kong
Hong Kong Model Yachting
Association
R. C. Eastwood,
2 Kelvin Tower,
18 MS Castle Peak Road,
New Territories,
Hong Kong.

(I) Italy
Modelvela Italia
Ceasare Brusotti
VL Masia,
46, 22100 Como
Italy.

(J) Japan
Japan Model Yacht Society (JMYS)
Ritsuri Honda,
2-16 Ote-Cho,
Takatsuki-Shi.
Osaka 569,
Japan.

(NZ) New Zealand
New Zealand Model Yachting
Association
David Watson,
20A Denver Grove,
Totara Park,
Upper Hutt,
New Zealand.

(N) Norway
Norsk Modellseilforening
Bjorn Nygaard,
Oreliveien 12C,
Oslo 5,
Norway.

(P) Portugal
Associacao Portuguese De Modelos A
Vela
Joao Figueirado,
URB.
Quinta Da Correia,
Cel.-G Lote
28-12 DRT Brandoa,
2700 Amadora,
Portugal.

(KS) Scotland
Scottish Model Yachting Association
R. W. Wishart,
28 London Street,
Edinburgh,
Scotland.

(SA) South Africa
Model Yacht Association of South
Africa
D. J. Fairbank,
52 Kew Avenue,
Westville, 3630,
Natal,
South Africa.

(E) Spain
Federacion Espanola De Modelismo
Naval
Narciso Claudio Ruiz,
Sebastian Elcano 19,
Seville 11,
Spain.

(S) Sweden
Svenska Modellseglarforbundet
(SMSF)
Jan Dejmo,
Krokslatts Parkgata 65B,
S-431 38 Molndal,
Sweden.

(Z) Switzerland
Association Suisse De Modelistes De
Bateaux (ASMB)
R. J. Savary,
Florissant 12,
1020-Renens,
Switzerland.

(US) USA
American Model Yachting Association
J. A. Davis,
PO Box 8,
Des Moines,
1A 50301-0008,
USA.

Hon. Gen. Sec.
K. Roberts,
51 Edinburgh Drive,
Prenton,
Birkenhead,
Merseyside.

Appendix Four
Model Power Boat Association Clubs

Scottish Sec.
Mrs F. Wilson
41 Bruce Avenue,
Inverness,
Glasgow

Ayr MBC
T. Walker
14 Blanefield Avenue,
Prestwick,
Scotland.

Edinburgh PBC
I. Greig
26 Corneby Bank Street.
Edinburgh,
EH4 1BB.

West Glasgow MBC
A. Weir
32 Moraine Circus,
Glasgow,
G15 6HE.

Highland MC
C. Kennedy
64 Inshes Crescent,
Inverness,
Scotland.

Glasgow MPBC
J. Patterson
68 Belstane Road,
Carluke,
Lanarkshire,
Scotland.

Irvine MC
J. Webb
20 Barnett Crescent,
Saltcoats,
Ayrshire,
Scotland.

Paisley MPBC
S. Wallwork
2 St. Fillans Drive,
Houston,
Renfrewshire,
Scotland.

Strathaven MS
A. Court
24 Orchard Gardens,
Strathaven,
Scotland.

North Ireland MPBC
A. Longman
4 Fendale Park,
Culleybackey,
Ballymena,
Co. Antrim,
Northern Ireland,
BT34 5PU.

NORTHERN AREA

Norhern Area Sec.,
J. A. Garnett
23 Durban Road,
Grimsby,
South Humberside,
DN32 8BD

Barrow SMS
I. Sharp
63 Black Butts Lane,
Barrow in Furness,
Cumbria LA14 3JZ.

Birkenhead MY&PBC
M. Allen
20 Kimberley Road,
Wallasey,
L45 7NU.

Bolton MBC
B. Aldous
506 Bolton Road West,
Ramsbotton,
Bury,
Lancs.

Bradford MES
T. Shaw
23 Derwent Road,
Bolton Road,
Bradford,
Yorks.

Bridlington MBC
R. A. Daniel
4 Lyth Close,
Bridlington,
East Yorks.

Bury Metro MMS
J. K. Taylor
14 Otterbury Close,
Bury,
Lancs.

Darlington MBC
J. Gavey
18 Glebe Road,
Darlington,
DL1 3D2.

Dewsbury MBC
R. Whitton
14 Woolgreaves Ave.,
Sandal,
Wakefield,
West Yorks.

Etherow MBC
E. Chesters
2 Southgate,
Heaton Chapel,
Stockport,
Cheshire.

Featherstone MBC
Mrs. Pashley
12 Cornwall Close,
Monck Bretton,
Nr.Barnsley,
S. Yorks.

Fiddlers Ferry MBC
Mrs. Warburton
4 Island Road,
Liverpool L19 1RL.

Hartlepool MBC
W. Cook
13 Lime Crescent,
Hartlepool,
Cleveland.

Halifax MBC
M. Galloway
34 Godfrey Road,
Halifax,
Yorks.

Harrogate & D.MBC
J. Kemp
25 Knapping Hill,
Harrogate,
West Yorks.

Heaton & D.MBC
A. Humpish
12 Willows Close,
Brunswick Green,
Wideopen,
Tyne and Wear.

Huddersfield MBC
V. Briggs
114 Balmoral Avenue,
Croosland Moor,
Huddersfield,
Yorks.

Hull MBC
J. Cherry
45 Hawthorne Avenue,
Anlaby Road,
Hull,
E. Yorks.

Keighley MBC
J. Barraclough
3 Lyndhurst Grove,
Allerton,
Bradford,
Yorks.

Killingworth MBC
K. Tweddle
36 Courtney Court,
Kingston Park,
Newcastle upon Tyne.

Kirklees MBC
D. Miller
86 Springfield Lane,
Morley,
Leeds,
Yorks.

Kirkby MBC
G. MacDonald
12 Makin Street,
Walton,
Liverpool 4.

Lancaster & M.MBC
M. Standing
Flat 9,
Gressingham House,
Hala Estate,
Lancaster, Lancs.

Leeds MBC
A. Midwinter
5 St. Annes Green,
Off St. Annes Drive,
Leeds.

Liverpool MPBC
N. Newbery
77 Muirhead Ave. East,
West Derby,
Liverpool 11.

Manchester RCMC
Miss Palmer
4 Dartington Close,
Baguley,
Manchester,
M23 9PW

Middleton MPBC
J. Whitehead
102 Warwick Road,
Middleton,
Manchester,
M24 1HY.

Nantwich MBC
Mrs Jackson
2 Hellath Wen,
Nantwich,
Cheshire.

Newton RCMS
F. G. Aitcheson
41 Hedge Hey,
Runcorn,
Cheshire.

Oldham MBC
I. Bay man
5 Jordan Avenue,
Shaw,
Lancs.

Rochdale MBC
R. Pilkington
2 West Avenue,
Smallbridge,
Rochdale,
Lancs.

South Shields MBC
A. Thompson
20 Borrowdale Avenue,
Seaburn Dene,
Sunderland,
Tyne and Wear.

Sheffield SMS
L. P. Grattan
209 Bannerdale Road,
Sheffield,
S11 9FB.

Sunderland MBC
A. Peterson
21 Alder Street,
Castleton,
Sunderland,
Tyne and Wear.

Teeside MBC
P. J. Farrow
30 Osprey Close,
Norton,
Stockton on Tees,
Cleveland.

Tynemouth MBC
R. A. Porrett
25 Thorntree Drive,
West Monkseaton,
Tyne and Wear.

Washington MBC
A. M. Egan
2 Doxford Cottages,
Hetton le Hole,
Tyne and Wear.

MIDLAND AREA

Midland Area Sec.
R. Don
55 Whiteoak Drive,
Finchfield,
Wolverhampton.

Bournville MBC
T. Cooper
41 Yateley Road,
Birmingham 15.

Burton & D. MBC
Mrs. Gall
114 Walford Road,
Rolleston,
Burton,
Staffs.

Cheltenham SME
B. Leath
16 Bibury Road,
Cheltenham,
Glos.

Cwmbran MBS
A. J. Greenham
22 Windsor Road,
Fairwater,
Gwent.

Cotswold MMC
R. Haines
43 Hanman Road,
Gloucester.

Coventry MBC
D. Tunnicliff
The Leys,
86 Bulkington Lane,
Nuneaton,
CV11 4SB.

Derby & D.MBC
G. Foster
16 Wilsthorpe Road,
Long Eaton,
Nottingham,
NG10 3JW.

Electra
D. Selby
Dolgornel,
Dolerw Drive,
Newtown,
Powys SY15 2HS.

Grantham MBC
M. R. Allsop
23 Hebden Walk,
Grantham,
Lincs.

Gwent MBC
Mrs Harris
82 Laurel Road,
Bassaleg,
Gwent NP1 9PL.

Hartsholme Elect.
P. Bilboa
22 Upper Saxon Street,
Lincoln.

Kingsbury Water Park
D. Thompson
126 Summefield Road,
Bolehall,
Tamworth,
Staffs.

Kings Lynn MBC
M. J. Howard
22 Fenland Road,
Ruffley Estate,
Kings Lynn,
Norfolk.

Leicester MBC
R. Folland
17 Highgate Avenue,
Birstall,
Leicester.

Lincoln MPBYC
J. W. North
71 St. Catherines Grove,
Lincoln.

Mansfield DMBC
N. Simmons
Lydene,
Howard Street,
Sutton in Ashfield,
Notts.

Milton Keynes MS
M. J. Kemp
4 Laurel Walk,
Kempston,
Beds.

Newent & D.MBC
F. Billingham
166 Whittern Way,
Hereford,
HR1 1PG.

N. Birmingham MPBC
W. J. Melvin
114 Newbolds Road,
Fallings Park,
Wolverhampton,
West Midlands,
WV10 0SF.

Northampton MBC
J. Ives
116 Derby Road,
Northampton,
NN1 4JS.

Nottingham MBC
S. Upton
37 Cambridge Road,
West Bridgeford,
Notts.

Orton MBC
G. Alexander
78 Pendleton,
Ravensthorpe,
Peterborough,
PE3 7LY.

Penarth MBC
H. Read
34 Ascot Close,
Trelai Park,
Cardiff,
S. Wales.

Peterborough IC
M. Szebeko
44 Pennington,
Orton Goldhay,
Peterborough,
Cambs.

Port Talbot MBC
C. Brooks
1 Ffrwo Villa,
Llangeinor,
Nr. Bridgend,
CF32 8PF.

Peterborough SC
R. Dean
53 Smallwood,
Ravensthorpe,
Cambs.

Potteries MBC
R. Barnes
2 Curtiss Place,
Meir Park,
Blythe Bridge,
Stoke on Trent.

Redditch MBC
L. C. Jones
51 Western Hill Close,
Astwood Bank,
Redditch.

Rushden MBC
J. Halfpenny
21 Lee Way,
Rauds,
Wellingborough,
Northants.

Scunthorpe MBC
J. Pank
123 Doncaster Road,
Scunthorpe,
S. Humberside.

Severn Gorge MM
B. Hughes
Flat 2,
47 Upper Barr,
Newport,
Salop.

Telford New Town
D. E. Warren
1 Talbot Close,
Wrockwardine Wood,
Telford,
Shropshire.

Whitchurch MBC
N. S. Tooker
27 Caxton Close,
New Whittington,
Chesterfield,
Derbys.

Wulfrana MBC
J. Golding
2 Vauxhall Gardens,
New Rowley Road,
Dudley,
Worcs.

Baggeridge MBC
R. Don
55 Whiteoak Drive,
Finchfield,
Wolverhampton.

Boston MBC
J. Burswell
23 Hardiway,
Boston,
Lincs.

SOUTHERN AREA

Southern Area Sec.
I. Folkson
25 Brook Way,
Chigwell,
Essex.

Ace MBC
M. Forsdyke
11 Bridge End,
Walthamstow,
London E17.

Acton & Ealing
R. Stonard
56 Aldbourne Road,
London W12.

Addelstone MBC
D. Watkins
7 Cobs Way,
New Haw,
Weybridge,
Surrey,

Alpha MBC
G. Colbeck
55 Sunningdale,
Luton,
Beds.

Andover MBC
R. Latimer
26 Colenzo Drive,
Andover,
Hants,
SP10 1JN.

Ass. Model Submariners
R. Serpell
25 Onslow Road,
Richmond,
Surrey.

Basildon MBC
P. Darch
29 High Road,
Vange,
Basildon,
Essex.

Basingstoke MBC
A. Wells
40 Aster Road,
Kempshott,
Basingstoke,
Hants.

Berrylands MBC
S. Kirby
244 Staines Road,
Twickenham,
Middx.

Bexley & D.MBC
D. Birkenshaw
268 Sherwood Park Avenue.,
Sidcup,
Kent.

Blackheath MBC
Tony Broad
1A Church Road,
Shortlands,
Bromley,
Kent.

Brighton MBC
V. Lassetter
74 Hangleton Way,
Hove,
Sussex.

Bromley MBC
K. Goodyer
27 Coniston Road,
Bromley,
Kent.

Bristol SMEE
W. H. Bosson
17 Knole Park,
Almondsbury,
Bristol.

Bristol Pegasus
B. Holder
35 Combermere,
Thornbury,
Bristol.

Buckaneers MC
D. Giles
64A Station Road,
Bow Brickhill,
Milton Keynes,
MK17 9JT.

Cambridge MBC
B. Lindsay
12 Church Close,
Cottenham,
Cambs.

Canterbury MBC
N. Ward
256 Beaver Road,
Ashford,
Kent.

Canvey Island
A. Baldry
7 Hyde Way,
Wickford,
Essex.

Crawley & D.MBC
M. Jennings
4 Burdock Close,
Broadfield,
Crawley,
Sussex.

Cygnets MBC
P. Bridgewater
22 Quickthorne Crescent,
Walderslade,
Chatham,
Kent ME5 0TL.

Eastbourne MBC
P. Ford
6 The Sanctuary,
Eastbourne,
Sussex.

East Essex Hydro
A. Cockman
31 Kensington Road,
Southend on Sea,
Essex.

Elmbridge MC
Mrs. Lidster
76 Stanley Gardens Road,
Teddington,
Middx.

Folkestone MBC
D. Honey
3 Walton Road,
Folkestone,
Kent.

Gipping Valley MBC
B. Davey
37 Colchester Road,
Ipswich,
Suffolk.

Gosport MBC
Mrs. Bullivant
8 Melville Road,
Gosport,
Hants.

Hanwell & D.MBC
L. Gross
16 Thurlestone Road,
Ruislip,
Middx.

Harrow SR
E. Allen
41 Ladyshot,
Harlow,
Essex.

Harrow Lodge MBC
P. Benzing
37 Albert Road,
Romford,
Essex.

Hampshire MHC
J. Hampton
71 Winter Road,
Southsea,
Hants.

Harrow & Wembley
A. B. Weait
12 Honister Close,
Stanmore,
Middx.

Hayle MBC
J. Lloyd
51 Fore Street,
Hayle,
Cornwall.

Herne Bay MBC
E. Eddington
42 St. Annes Drive,
Herne Bay,
Kent.

Hertford DMS
D. Metcalf
1 Wentworth Cotts,
Haultwick,
Dane End,
Nr. Ware,
Herts.

Highgate MBC
J. B. Stevenson
Flat C,
24 Belsize Park Gardens,
London NW3

High Wycombe MBC
J. D. Elphick
102 Suffield Road,
High Wycombe,
Bucks.

Hustlers
R. A. Palmer
5 St. Davids Close,
Cox Green,
Maidenhead,
Berks.

Hydroplane C
A. Wall
281 Fairfax Road,
West Heath,
Birmingham.

Kingfishers MBC
R. Thayne
122 Sheepwalk,
Shepperton,
Middx.

Leighton Buzzard MBC
H. J. Faunch
117 Meadow Way,
Leighton Buzzard,
Beds.

Lydd MMC
A. G. Greenfield
84/86 London Road,
Teynham,
Nr. Sittingbourne,
Kent.

Mayesbrook MBC
E. Percival
741 Becontree Avenue,
Dagenham,
Essex.

Medway MMS
R. Lewis
282 Meirscourt Road,
Rainham,
Gillingham,
Kent.

Morton SME
G. Turner
13 Clay Avenue,
Mitcham,
Surrey.

Mid Thames MBC
J. H. Cripps
91 Tern Close,
Tilehurst,
Reading,
RG5 4AZ.

Mid Essex & Suffolk
Mrs. Stokes
46 Meadow View Road,
Sudbury,
Suffolk.

Moorhen MBC
D. Austen
The Rise,
Takeley Street,
Nr. Bishops Stortford,
Herts.

N. London SME
T. Hammer
19 Marion Road,
Mill Hill,
London NW7.

Newbury & D.
P. M. Annal
40 2nd Avenue,
Ravens Wing Park,
Aldermaston,
Reading, Berks.

New Clapham MBC
E. Diboll
70 Kimberley Road,
Beckenham,
Kent.

Norfolk and Norwich
P. Goodson
49 Anthony Drive,
Norwich,
NR3 4EW.

OMRA
A. Baldry
7 Hyde Way,
Wickford,
Essex.

Oxford MBC
D. Swain
31 Beech Croft Road,
Oxford,
OX2 7AY

Parkway MBC
A. Woolidge
39 Parkway,
Camden Town,
London NW1 7PN

Portsmouth MBC
D. L. Thorne
25 Fifth Street,
Fratton,
Portsmouth,
Hants.

Plymouth MBC
C. J. Sells
62 Tangmere Avenue,
Ernesettle,
Plymouth.

Saracens MBC
M. Tidmarsh
35 Athlone Road,
Tulse Hill,
London SW2 3DT.

St. Albans MES
P. Lambert
371 Barton Road,
Streatley,
Luton,
Beds.

S. M. Shipwrights
A. Locks
Squerrys,
1 Haven Close,
Istead Rise,
Meopham,
Kent.

Southampton MBC
R. Stockton
49 Obelisk Road,
Woolston,
Southampton,
Hants.

Southend MBC
D. Hallam
12 Meesons Mead,
Rochford,
Essex.

Southsea MSSC
M. J. Palmer
39 Ranelagh Road,
Stamshaw,
Portsmouth,
Hants.

Stevenage MBC
Mrs. A. Williams
489 Canterbury Way,
Stevenage,
Herts.

Swindon MBC
M. Fortune
10 Rose Street,
Swindon,
Wilts.

Thames Valley MBC
P. Martin
13 Northern Road,
Slough,
Bucks.

Tunbridge Wells MBC
A. G. Smith
184 Broadmead,
Tunbridge Wells,
Kent.

Tonbridge & D.
D. E. Lane
88 Lavender Hill,
Tonbridge,
Kent.

Tone Vale MBC
E. Grant
3 Eastleigh Road,
Taunton,
Somerset.

Torbay MBC
B. Garner
Mount Kennedy,
Parkham Road,
Brixham,
S. Devon.

Victoria MBC
N. G. Phelps
17 Jersey Road,
Leytonstone,
London E11

Water & Wheels
R. J. Fuller
183A St. Mary's Lane,
Upminster,
Essex.

Welwyn G.C.SME
M. Peers
53 Aldykes,
Hatfield,
Herts.

Wessex MBC
P. Dunbar
169 Barrack Road,
Christchurch,
Dorset.

Westward Offs. MPBRA
T. Ellis
124 Torridge Avenue,
Shiphay,
Torquay,
Devon.

Wood Green MBC
A. F. Miles
5 Courcy Road,
London N8 0QH.

Worthing MBC
P. Bacon
17 Tavy Close,
Durrington,
Worthing,
Sussex.

Yate & Sodbury
D. Battson
22 Spar Road,
Yate,
Bristol.

Yeovil & District
F. Miller
12 Nash Lane,
Yeovil,
Somerset.

Gravesend MMES
H. A. Townsend
13 Rosedale Close,
Stone,
Dartford,
Kent.

M.P.B.A. Natinal Hon. Gen. Sec.
G. Metcalf
Broad Meads, Ware,
Herts.

Appendix Five
Propeller Suggestions

Choice of a propeller for intial trials can be puzzling. The following are suggested diameters for standard pitch propellers available commercially which should offer a reasonable starting point for average models. It is desirable to experiment with the next size up or down, or with lower or greater pitch, in order to establish the best propeller(s) for a particular combination of model and motor.

ELECTRIC

Watts	2-blade		3-blade		Approx. shaft size
	in.	mm	in.	mm	
5	7/8	—	3/4	—	2mm-3/32in.
10	1-1¼	30	1-1⅛	30	3/32in.-4BA
15	1¼-1½	30-40	1¼-1⅜	30-35	4BA
20	1½-1¾	40-45	1½	40	4BA
30	1¾-2	45-50	1¾	45	4BA
50	2-2½	50-65	1¾-2¼	45-60	4BA-2BA

DIESEL

c.c.	cu. in.	Average sport model		Fast model		Approx. shaft size
		in.	mm	in.	mm	
0·5	0·03	1	30	1	25-30	4BA
0·8	0·049	1-1¼	30	1-1¼	30	4BA
1·0	0·06	1¼-1⅜	30-35	1¼	30-35	4BA
1·5	0·09	1⅜-1½	35-40	1¼-1⅜	30-35	4BA
2·5	0·15	1½-1¾	40-45	1⅜-1½	35-40	4BA
3·5	0·21	1½-2	50-50	1⅜-1¾	35-45	4BA-2BA
5·0	0·29	1¾-2¼	45-55	1¾-2	45-50	2BA

GLOW

c.c.	cu. in.	in.	mm	in.	mm	Approx. shaft size
0·8	0·049	¾-⅞	—	¾-⅞	—	4BA
1·0	0·06	1-1¼	30	⅞-1¼	30	4BA
1·5	0·09	1⅛-1⅜	30-35	1⅛-1⅜	30-35	4BA
2·5	0·15	1¼-1½	35	1¼-1⅜	30-35	4BA
3·5	0·21	1⅜-1½	35-40	1⅜-1½	35-40	2BA
5·0	0·29	1½-2	40-50	1½-1¾	40-45	2BA
6·5	0·40	2-2¼	50-55	1¾-2	45-50	2BA
10·0	0·61	2¼-2½	55-65	2-2½	50-65	2BA

Notes.
1. Figures can only be a guide, since power or running speed of engines vary considerably and weight and type of hull, resistance etc, affect propeller performance.
2. Plain or standard pitch is approx. 1·2-1·3×diameter, average high or X pitch 1.4-1.6×diameter.
3. 4BA is ·142in., approx. 3·5mm, 2BA is ·185in., approx. 4·5mm, referring to diameter of plain (i.e. unthreaded) shaft.

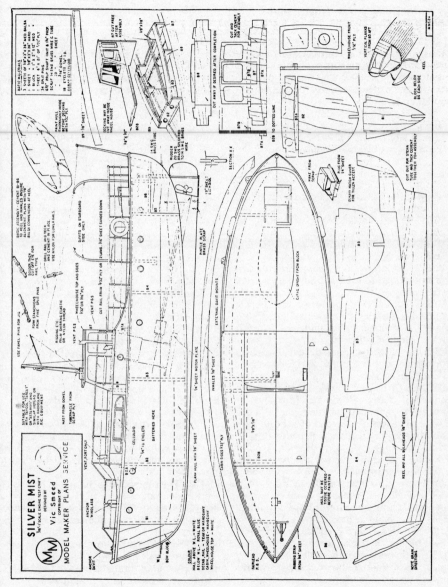

Example of a structural plan for a scale-type power model.

Glossary

Some of the commoner nautical terms, full-size and model.

ABOUT, TO GO – To turn a beating vessel through the wind on to the opposite tack.

AFT (ABAFT, AFTER) – Towards the stern or rear.

AIRSCOOP – A simple type of ventilator for small craft.

AMIDSHIP ('MIDSHIP) – Central.

APRON – Reinforcement timber bolted to aft face of stem, also a shorter member joining chine members at their bow ends.

BACK-LASH – Taking up of play in gears by back pressure.

BACKSTAY – Line leading down from the mast to brace it from aft.

BAFFLE – A perforated plate set in the fuel tank, etc., to reduce liquid surge.

BALLAST – Extra weight usually in the form of lead added to bring a boat to its correct waterline.

BALLOON JIB – A very large headsail, sometimes used on a racing yacht.

BARBETTE – Circular mounting for gun turret or other rotating fitting.

BARQUE – A three masted vessel square-rigged on fore and main, and fore and aft rigged on mizzen.

BARQUENTINE – A three masted vessel square-rigged on foremast, fore and aft rigged on main and mizzen.

BEAM – The greatest width of a boat, also one of the timbers on which the deck is laid.

BEATING – Sailing towards the wind on a tack or tack-and-tack.

BELAY – To make fast a rope, to stop.

BELAYING PIN – A brass or wooden pin set in a pin rail for securing running rigging.

BEND – To fasten in place.

BERMUDA RIG – Triangular sail(s) with luff held to mast by jackline etc.

BILGE – The portion of the hull below water, also the inside of the hull where extraneous water collects.

BINNACLE – A container for a ship's compass.

BLOCK – A pulley which is used in rigging.

BLUSHING – Whitening of cellulose liquids due to chemical reaction with water vapour on drying.

BOAT – Formerly a vessel built on bent frames (a ship used sawn frames), but nowadays any vessel which is capable of being hoisted aboard another vessel; except in the R.N., generally applied to any vessel at all.

BOAT CHOCKS – Wood cradles for stowing a boat.

BOLLARD – Sturdy posts normally set in pairs for making off cables, etc.

BOLT ROPE – A rope sewed to the edge of a sail for strengthening.

BOOM – A spar extending a sail.

BOOT TOP – A painted line or changing colour at the hull water line.

BOTTLESCREW – Tensioning device capable of shortening or lengthening by screw adjustment.

BOW – The forward part of a vessel.

BOWLINE – Strictly the buttock lines of a hull drawing are bowlines forward of midships and buttock lines aft. Also line used to haul forward the weather leach of a square sail when sailing close to the wind. Also a knot.

BOWSIE (BOWSER) – A small slide used in a model's rigging.

BOWSPRIT – A spar projecting forward of the bow from which headsails are set.

BRACE – A line leading up from the yard arms to control the yard position horizontally.

BRAIL – The rope used to assist the furling of a fore and aft sail.

BREAD AND BUTTER – Hull construction using a number of planks laminated together.

BREASTHOOK – A reinforcing member joining the inwales at the bow.

BRIDLE – A short line attached at two points to tether a model for running.

BRIG – A two masted square-rigged vessel.

BRIGANTINE – A two masted vessel square-rigged on the foremast, and fore and aft rigged on the main.

BROACH – Sudden loss of control with slewing 90° across immediate course. Also a polygonal tool for enlarging holes.

BULKHEAD – An internal solid frame dividing the ship.

BULLSEYE – A circular block grooved round its edge, and pierced through the centre for ropes.

BULWARK – The sides of the vessel above deck level.

BUNT – The centre of the square sail.

BUSH – A metal bearing.

BUTTOCK – The convexity of the lower stern, also a line, parallel to the centre line in plan, showing the shape of the plane cut by the line in profile.

CABLE LAID – A rope in which three hawser-laid ropes are laid up right to left.

CAM – A rotating disc bearing against an arm, and shaped so that the arm is raised or lowered at certain points of rotation.

CAMBER – The thwartship curve of a deck.

CAPSTAN – A drum revolving vertically, used for hauling in a rope, etc.

CARAVEL – A three masted vessel similar to a galleon, but considerably smaller.

CARLING – Fore and aft beam between two or more deck beams.

CATALYST – A chemical reagent which when mixed with other materials starts an irreversible chemical change.

CENTREBOARD – The fin keel which can be raised or lowered in a well to provide additional side area for shallow draft boats.

CENTRE OF GRAVITY – The point through which the weight of the boat may be said to act.

CHAIN PIPE – A casting set in the deck through which the anchor chain passes into the chain locker.

CHAIN PLATE – A fitting for the attachment of the main mast shrouds at their lower ends.

CHAMFER – An angle planed into a piece of timber, out of square with the main faces.

CHINAMAN – Elastic line biasing a model yacht's mainboom to preferred side.

CHINE – The line where the side of the boat meets the bottom, forming a sharp angle.

CLEAT – A fitting with two horns for making fast a rope.

CLEW – The lower corner of a square sail, or the aft corner of a fore and aft sail.

CLINCHER BUILT – A method of planking where the lower edge of each plank overlaps the upper edge of the plank below.

CLIPPER – A three or four mast square-rig vessel employing a very narrow beam hull.

COAMING – A raised structure round a hatchway or cockpit to prevent water entering.

COMPANIONWAY – A stairway leading down from the main deck.

COMPRESSION IGNITION – A type of internal combustion engine in which combustion is effected by the heat generated by compression of gases.

CONVECTION COOLING – A method of cooling an engine by means of a water header tank, employing the natural tendency of warmed water to rise, thus producing circulation.

COUNTER – The overhang of the stern.

COURSE – The main sail on a square-rigged mast, also a moving ship's heading.

CRINGLE – A loop of rope spliced into the edge of a sail.

CROSSJACK – The lowest yard on the mizzen mast.

CROSS-TREES – Light timbers to spread the rigging of a mast.

CROSS-SECTION – A true section of a hull, etc., at any point looking along the longitudinal axis.

CRYSTAL – Fine sliver of quartz ground to resonate at fixed frequency.

CUTWATER – The part of the stem on the actual water line

CUTTER – Formerly a single masted vessel carrying a square sail and a boom mainsail, topsail and gaff topsail; nowadays normally fore and aft rigged.

DAGGER PLATE – Vertical fin approximately amidships to reduce leeway and/or increase speed of turn.

DAVIT – A type of small crane for hoisting and lowering ships' boats.

DEADEYE – A wooden block grooved round the periphery, and equipped with three holes to pass ropes.

DEADRISE – The angle of a ship's bottom from the horizontal.

DEADWOOD – Normally the solid wood part of a keel.

DECK PIPE – The upper lip of the anchor hawse pipes.

DISPLACEMENT – The weight of the volume of water displaced by a boat, i.e. the weight of the boat itself.

DRAFT (DRAUGHT) – The distance between the waterline and the lowest point of the keel.

DOUBLER – Reinforcing member secured to and alongside a structural part, e.g. keel.

DOWEL – Timber in strips of circular section.

DYNAMIC LIFT – Lift force opposing gravity created by forward movement of hull in water.

EARING – A rope used in bending a sail, particularly at the corners of a square sail.

EGG-BOX CONSTRUCTION – A method of building where structural members are all halved together.

EYEBOLT – A bolt with a loose ring in its head.

EYEPLATE – A small plate incorporating an eye used in securing or passing a line.

FAIRLEAD – A fitting for guiding a rope.

FALL – A rope which with blocks comprises a tackle, e.g. boat falls as fitted to davits.

FASHION PIECE – Shaped block at bow or stern of (usually slender) hull.

FEATHER EDGE – A timber which is tapered off to a knife edge along one side.

FLANGE – A rim projecting at right angles.

FLEMISH COIL – A coil of rope in which each coil lies flat, giving the appearance of a mat.

FLYING JIB – The outermost headsail.

FOOTING – Speed through water, especially to windward.

FOOT-ROPE – A rope mounted on a square yard on which to stand.

FORE (FORWARD) – Towards the bow.

FORE AND AFT – From stem to stern; along the longitudinal axis.

FORECASTLE – Space beneath the forward portion of the deck, usually abbreviated to fo'c'sl.

FOREFOOT – The point where the stem meets the keel.

FOREMAST – The mast nearest the bow.

FORESTAY – A stay running down from the mast, and made to brace the mast against backward stresses.

FRAME – A thwartship structural member of the hull.

FULCRUM – The point about which rotation takes place.

FURL – To bunch up and secure sails.

FUTTOCK – A portion of a frame; in a ship each frame usually comprises six to eight futtocks.

GAFF – A spar on the afterside of the mast supporting the head of a fore and aft sail.

GAFF TOPSAIL – A triangular sail filling in the space between the gaff and the top mast.

GALLEON – 15th, 16th or 17th century sailing vessel, notable for a high poop.

GALLOWS FRAME – Framework carrying a platform for stowing boats, etc., above deck level.

GANGWAY – An opening in the bulwarks.

GANGWAY LADDER – (ACCOMMODATION LADDER) – Steps leading down the ship's side.

GARBOARD STRAKE – The plank next to the keel.

GASKET – A rope wound round the furled sail; a relatively soft packing piece between two joined surfaces.

GENOA – Form of jib of large size, clew of which extends aft of mast. Not widely used in models due to difficulty of changing tack.

GOOSENECK – A swivel joint by which the heel of a boom is held to the mast.

GOVERNOR – A mechanism fitted to some motors to limit the maximum speed.

G.R.P. – Glass-reinforced plastic, normally glass cloth or mat set in polyester resin.

GUDGEON – An eye in which a rudder pintle turns.

GUNWALE – The top-most edge of the deck, or a small boat rail.

GUY – A line used to steady a spar.

GUYING – Carrying out a gye.

GYBE – A change of course relative to the wind when running, with the main boom swinging to the opposite side.

GYE – To change tack intentionally when sailing to windward; also the mechanism used to change tack.

HALLIARD (HALYARD) – The rope used to hoist sails or yards, etc.

HATCH – An opening in the deck; the cover for such an opening.

HAWSE PIPE – The pipe emerging in the side of the bow through which the anchor chain passes.

HAWSER – A heavy rope.

HAWSER LAID A rope in which the strands run to the right.

HEAD – The top or outboard end, e.g. mast head, etc.; the top side or corner of a sail.

HEADSAILS – Fore and aft sails forward of the foremast.

HEEL – The bottom or inboard end, e.g. mast heel; the canted angle at which a vessel sails.

HELM – The tiller or steering mechanism.

HOUNDS – A mast fitting carrying cross trees, etc.

HORSE – A thwartship rail to which a model's sheets are hooked.

IDLER GEAR – A small gear doing no work, but reversing the rotation of a second gear.

INTERNAL COMBUSTION ENGINE – Any engine deriving its power from the expansion of gases burned internally.

IRONS ('IN IRONS') – When a boat comes up into wind and will not pay off, she is in irons. The condition is accompanied by sail-shaking, etc.

JACK LINE – A taut line on which a sail is bent.

JAWS – A type of wooden crutch at the heel of a boom engaging the mast.

JIB – A triangular sail set on a stay forward of the mast.

JIB BOOM – A spar extending beyond the bowsprit; the spar attached to the foot of a model yacht jib.

JIG – An internal or external structural member. assuring accurate alignment.

JIGGER – A small fore and aft sail on the after mast of a yawl, etc.

JOGGLING – The irregular jointing of deck planks into a kingplank or other plank running in a different direction.

JUMPER STRUT – A strut used to extend a backstay.

KEDGE – A type of light anchor.

KEEL – The backbone of a vessel.

KEELSON – The heavy timber fitted to the keel for reinforcement.

KETCH – A two masted vessel with a small after mast stepped forward of the rudder post.

KILN-DRYING – A process of baking timber in a kiln to dry off sap.

KINGPLANK – The central plank of the deck running fore and aft.

KITCHEN RUDDER – A device consisting of two cups fitting round the propeller, and adjustable for steering or for speed control and movement astern.

LAMINATE – To build up in several layers bonded together.

LANYARD – A light rope for making anything fast.

LARBOARD – Disused term for port side.

LATEEN – A large triangular sail set at an angle to the mast.

LEACH – The after edge of a fore and aft sail; the sides of a square sail.

LEE – Area of reduced wind downwind of ship or object caused by wind shadow. Also downwind side of vessel or object.

LEEWARD – Downwind, i.e. opposite the direction from which the wind is blowing.

LEEWAY – Sideways component of vessel's movement arising from being blown down wind.

LIFT – A rope attached to the end of a spar supporting its weight and determining its vertical position.

LIVERPOOL BOY – A light rubber band on an adjustable line, attached to a jib-boom and tending to keep the jib on one tack.

LOOF – That part of a ship where the beam narrows towards the stern.

LUFF – The forward edge of a fore and aft sail; to allow a vessel to come up to the wind.

LUFFING – Bringing the head of a vessel nearer the wind.

MAIN MAST – The middle of a three masted vessel, or after mast of a two master, except a yawl or ketch where it is the forward mast.

MAINSAIL – The largest sail on the main mast.

MARK – A buoy or other easily visible object (pole etc.) indicating course to be followed.

MIZZEN MAST – The after mast.

MOCK-UP – To make a dummy non-working model in the same size as the finished prototype.

MULTI-RACING – Racing of a number of model power boats (often 6-8) simultaneously.

NAVIGA – International organising body for, principally, model power boats, recognised by many countries.

NICAD – Abbreviation for 'nickel-cadmium cell' widely used in radio equipment and electric-powered models.

O.D. – Outside Diameter. (I.D. is Inside Diameter).

PARREL – A band or strap securing a yard to a mast, but allowing the yard to be moved up and down.

PAWL – A pivoted lever engaging in pockets in a wheel, preventing the wheel from moving back.

PAY OFF – To turn away from the wind.

PEAK – The tip of a gaff, or the corner of a sail attached thereto; the speed at which maximum power is produced by an engine.

PINTLE – The pin fitted to a rudder to provide a hinge movement.

PLATE AND BULB – A keel consisting of a thin plate, swelling out at the bottom for the lead.

PLUG – Shaped male pattern from which a mould (occasionally a finished shell) can be made. Also, of course, a bung or a male electrical connector.

POOP – The raised deck at the after end of the vessel; in the navy, the quarter deck.

PORT – The left-hand side of a ship; an opening in the side of a hull or deck.

QUADRANT – A segment of a circle; a navigational instrument.

QUARTER – The side of the vessel between stern and the attachment point of the after rigging.

RAKE – The angle of the mast from the vertical, the angle of the stem or transom.

RATLINE – Small ropes passing across shrouds to form a ladder.

REEF – To reduce sail area.

REEVE – To run a line through a hole

RESIN BONDED – Glued together by means of a water and heat proof resin glue.

RIB AND PLANK – A hull built by planking on to ribs which remain part of the finished structure.

ROUND BILGE – A boat in which turn of the bilge is a continual curve.

RUBBING STRAKE (RUBBER) – A fore and aft timber laid externally to protect the planking.

RUNNING LIGHTS (STEAMING LIGHTS) – Lights carried on each side of a vessel in motion, red to port and green to starboard.

RUNNING RIGGING – Lines for setting sails etc., which are moved from time to time, standing rigging is the permanent bracing, etc. for masts.

SCARF – A joint between two pieces of timber, blending them into one.

SCHNORKEL – A device which can be surfaced by a submerged submarine, through which air may be drawn into the boat.

SCHOONER – A fore and aft rigged vessel with anything from two to seven masts. A topsail schooner is two masted carrying a square top and top gallant sail on the fore.

SEIZE – To bind with light cord.

SCUPPER – A drain cut through a bulwark.

SELVEDGE – The manufactured edge of cloth.

SERVO – Electro-mechanical device converting radio signals into physical movement.

SHACKLE – A U-shaped iron fitting with a pin closing the open end.

SHARPIE – A hard chine boat.

SHEAVE – The grooved wheel in a block.

SHEER – The curve of a deck viewed from abeam.

SHEET – The rope attached to the clew of a sail.

SHIP – Strictly a three or four mast vessel, square-rigged on all masts.

SHOCK MOUNTING – Mounting on rubber, etc., so that vibration, etc. is not transmitted to the fitting.

SHROUD-LAID – Rope of four strands laid to right round fifth strand (the 'heart').

SIGNAL GENERATOR – A piece of wireless apparatus, comparison with which enables a transmitter's frequency to be determined.

SKIN – The covering of planking forming the sides and bottom of the hull.

SKYLIGHT – A window over a cabin, etc.

SLOOP – A single masted fore and aft rigged vessel.

SNOWBRIG – Rig distinguished by having separate mast parallel and adjacent to mainmast to which the trysail (fore and aft) is rigged.

SOLENOID – An iron core which is withdrawn into a wire coil when the coil is electrically energised.

SPANKER – The fore and aft sail on the mizzen mast.

SPAR – A yard, gaff or boom.

SPINNAKER – A large triangular sail set on a boom on the opposite side of the mast to the main boom, and used when running.

SPREADER – A strut extending from the cross-trees to spread the backstays.

SPRITSAIL – A square sail set beneath the bowsprit.

SQUARE-RIGGED – Equipped with square sails the yards of which are thwartship.

STANCHION – The vertical pillars carrying rails, etc.

STARBOARD – The right side of the boat looking forward.

STAY – A heavy rope used to brace a mast.

STEM – The foremost timber in a hull.

STERN – The after end of a ship.

STERN POST – A vertical timber joined to the after end.

STERN SHEETS – The space in the stern of the small boat.

STOCK – The shaft of a rudder. Also the straight cross-piece at the top of an anchor, often omitted in modern designs such as Wasteney-Smith's stockless anchor.

STRAKE – A plank running the length of the hull.

STRINGER – A light structural member running fore and aft.

STROPPING – Encircling a block with a rope.

STUFFING BOX – A short bearing through which a propeller shaft emerges from the hull.

SUPERSTRUCTURE – The part of a boat above deck level.

SWEAT – To run solder through a joint by means of a blowlamp, etc.

TACK – The lower forward corner of a fore and aft sail; the rope that holds down the forward clew of a square sail when on the wind; the identification of a vessel's course relative to the wind/set of her sails – starboard tack when the wind is on the starboard side. To tack is to bring the vessel's head through the wind so that it then blows on the opposite side.

TACKLE – Gear composed of blocks and rope.

TAFFRAIL – A rail round the stern.

TEMPLATES – A pattern cut to check the shape.

THROAT – The forward upper corner of the fore and aft sail.

THWART – A small boat seat.

THWARTSHIP – From side to side.

TILLER – A bar connected to the rudder head and moved from side to side.

TIMBERHEAD – Part of the frame projecting above deck against which the bulwarks are built.

TOP HAMPER – The rigging, etc., above deck.

TOPPING LIFT – A tackle holding up the end of a boom or yard.

TOPSIDES – The sides of the hull above the waterline.

TRANSOM – The flat, usually upright, stern of a boat.

TRAVELLER – A ring or pulley sliding across a horse.

TRENNALS – Wooden pegs (treenails) used, particularly, for securing planking in lieu of nails etc. In models, tiny dowels, almost splinters, of hard wood.

TRIM TAB – Adjustable plate affecting vessel's attitude or course. On power boats, often one either side of transom flush with hull bottom adjustable for horizontal angle. On yachts, usually vertical at trailing edge of fin (sometimes also leading edge) to produce sideways 'lift' opposing leeway.

TRUNK – Basically a surrounding structure, specifically in models the tube through which passes the rudder stock.

TUMBLEHOME – The inward slope of the topsides.

TURNBUCKLE – A screw device for tightening rigging.

VANE GEAR – A device used to steer a model at a constant angle to the wind.

VANG – A rope steadying the outer end of a gaff.

WAIST – The mid portion of the deck.

WALE – A heavy strake running fore and aft.

WATERLINE – The line at which a vessel rides when afloat.

WATERWAY – A channel running round the deck serving as a gutter.

WATT – Measure of work (746 watts=1 h.p.) obtained by multiplying intensity of current and electromotive force, i.e. amps× volts.

WEAR – To change tack while running.

WEATHER – Upwind (e.g. sailing to weather), that part of a vessel or object against which the wind is blowing (weather side), in the direction from which the wind is blowing (weather shore, weather mark, etc.).

WHIP – A single block fitted with a line; the springiness natural to timber, etc.

WINCH – An engine fitted with a drum for holding a rope.

WINDLASS – A mechanical device for hoisting an anchor.

WINDWARD – Towards the wind, into wind (interchangeable with 'weather' above).

WORM – To lay thin twine between the strands of a rope to present a smooth surface; a gear used when considerable reduction in speed is required.

XEBEC – Lateen rigged Mediterranean vessel.

YARD – A horizontal spar from which a square sail is set.

YARD ARM – The outer eighth of a yard.

YAWL – A fore and aft rig consisting of two masts, the after one being very small and stepped behind the sternpost.